Kaye Wood's

STRIP-CUT QUILTS

using the 4-angle of the Starmaker 8
Master Template

another book in the *Strip Like A Pro* program,
made up of all of the Strip Quilting books, videos,
Starmaker Master Templates, and quilting tools
by

Kaye Wood

Published by

Krause Publications
700 E. State St.
Iola, WI 54990-0001
(715) 445-2214
www.krause.com

Please call or write for our free catalog of publications. Our toll-free number to place an order or obtain a free catalog is (800) 258-0929 or please use our regular business telephone (715) 445-2214 for editorial comment and further information.

Library of Congress Catalog Number 00-111279
ISBN 0-87349-258-7

Some products in this book are registered trademarks: Starmaker®, View-A-Strip™, View-A-Square™, View & Do™ Shapes (Hexa-Cut™, Octa-Cut™), Static Sticker™, and Perfect Miter™.

All photography by Kris Kandler of Krause Publications; illustrations by Kaye Wood; cover design by Mary Lou Marshall; page design by Marilyn Hochstatter; and editing by Maria L. Turner.

Kaye Wood

You can learn to Strip Like A Pro!

Just follow along with Kaye as she shows you how to simplify both the cutting and the piecing of quilts so your quiltmaking can be more fun, easier, and more accurate. Forget all those sizes of templates; you only need the Starmaker 8 Master Template for all the quilts in this book.

A lot of the quilting techniques that Kaye teaches are easy enough for beginners, but they don't look like beginner projects. That's the fun part for her. The best quilts for a beginner to start with are the "pointless designs." Kaye started to develop and include these designs when she realized that not everyone wants to match points. It is much more important to enjoy the creative process, so some of you have to accept the fact that you are one of the "pointless people" and leave the pointed designs for the "pointed people."

Kaye's *Strip Like A Pro* program is made up of her strip quilting books, videos, three Starmaker Master Templates, and several quilting tools—View-A-Strip, the View-A-Square and the View & Do Shapes (circles, squares, Hexa-Cut, and Octa-Cut) for fussy-cutting.

Starmaker Master Templates

Kaye is especially well-known for her three Starmaker Master Templates, which revolutionized the way lots of quilts are made. The Starmaker Master Template concept has enabled even beginners to make quilts that traditionally took much more skill than Kaye's techniques. The Master Templates are used to strip cut more than 150 different quilt patterns; in fact, most geometric quilt patterns can be strip-pieced using one of the angles or half-angles on the Master Templates.

Spools of Lace, made by Kaye Wood. Directions on page 32.

Since 1978, Kaye has taught her strip quilting techniques internationally. In 1988, a friend asked her when she was going to teach her ideas through television. She thought, "Why not?" and now has the longest running quilting shows on TV—*Strip Quilting, Quilting for the '90s* and *Kaye's Quilting Friends*. In 2000, Kaye completed her 28th season and 364th program for public television. She has also appeared as a guest on several national sewing/quilting/craft TV shows.

Before quilting, Kaye taught clothing construction, pattern drafting and machine embroidery. One day, one of her machine embroidery students asked if she would teach them to make a quilt. Kaye said, "Why not? Next week, bring three half-yard pieces of fabric." And that was the beginning of the first quilting class she taught. The rest is history.

Table of Contents

Tablerunner Trio; see page 17.

Scrap Happy; see page 23.

Glacier Ice; see page 34.

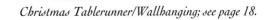

Christmas Tablerunner/Wallhanging; see page 18.

Introduction

Rosebud Baby Quilt, made by Kaye Wood. Directions on page 25.

Kaye Wood's Strip-Cut Quilts

Fabric Preparation

Fabric should be washed and dried before using. Just before washing, I cut the four corners off my fabric; this reduces raveling, but most of all, it tells me my fabric has been washed and dried when I later go to use it. Washing and drying fabric removes the sizing, and it reduces the possibility of shrinkage and color bleeding.

Measuring Accurately

Always use the same ruler to cut the width of your strips within any one project. Rulers are not always the same; changing from one ruler to another can result in strips that are not cut the same width. By using the same ruler, your measurements will be more accurate.

Most of the strips used in the designs in this book are cut across the width of the fabric (40 to 44 inches) from selvedge to selvedge. Fabrics with an interesting lengthwise design, such as a stripe, can be cut with the design or across the width.

The View-A-Strip tool can help you decide which way will be more effective.

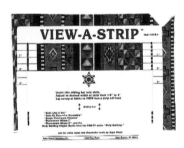

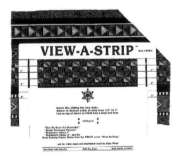

The View-A-Strip tool helps you view strips of varying widths accurately. Here, the tool views a 2 1/4-inch strip on material laid horizontally, and a 2-inch strip on a vertical design.

Cutting Accurately

When rotary cutting, always cut away from you and move the cutter in only one direction. Do not cut back and forth.

To cut strips with the rotary cutter: fold the fabric in half with selvedges together. Lay the folded fabric on the rotary cutting mat. Smooth the fabric out so it lays flat, even if the selvedges don't line up exactly.

Cut the fabric perpendicular (at right angles) to the fold to straighten one edge, using the rotary cutter and a heavy ruler. Fold the fabric once more by bringing the

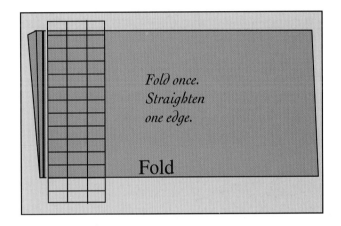

Fold once. Straighten one edge.

Fold

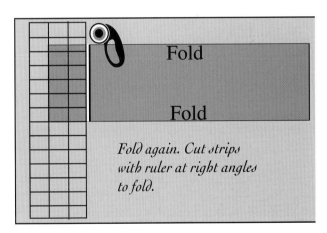

Fold

Fold

Fold again. Cut strips with ruler at right angles to fold.

folded edge to the selvedge. The fabric will now be in four layers and the shorter length will be easier to cut. Every third or fourth cut, unfold the fabric to check to see that your strips are straight.
Cut the strips needed, using the lines on a ruler to cut accurate strips. For example, to

cut 1 1/2-inch wide strips, place the 1 1/2-inch line on the ruler at the cut edge of the fabric. Cut along the edge of the ruler with the rotary cutter.

Make sure the blades are sharp. Dull blades are harder to use and they force the fabric down into the mat causing it to look fuzzy.

Sewing Accurately

Sewing accurately is very important. All your seam allowances should be the same width, preferably a scant 1/4 inch. The size given for each project listed in this book assumes that you will be using a scant (or quilters) 1/4-inch seam allowance. If your seam allowances are wider, that's okay, but your designs will be slightly smaller than the given measurements. For best results, use a 1/4-inch foot or some type of seam guide on your sewing machine. For strip piecing, it is always a good idea to shorten the stitch length to about 2 centimeters, or 10 stitches per inch.

Pressing Accurately

Pressing correctly is important in all kinds of patchwork, and it becomes even more important when you work with angles in your designs.

Seam allowances are usually pressed to one side in patchwork, but before pressing the seam allowances toward one side, press—up and down without sliding the iron—the seamline in the position it was sewn. This will help to keep the stitches locked in the center of the fabric. In some cases, especially when several seam allowances come together, it may be best to press the seams open.

Accurate pressing is ensured by:
1. Pressing with the grain.
Whenever possible, move the iron with the grain of the fabric. Ironing can stretch fabric if it goes along the crosswise grain of the fabric. For instance, moving the iron along the length of the strip will stretch it.

2. Pressing from the right side of the fabric.
Pressing from the wrong side can result in pleats forming at the seamline. Instead set the iron on the right side of the first strip, hold the rest of the strips up in the air. As you slide the iron from the first strip to the next, the seam allowances will be pressed in the right direction.

3. No steam.
Pressing with steam will stretch the fabric.

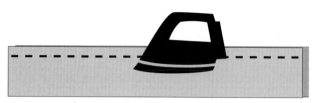

1. Press the seamline as it was sewn

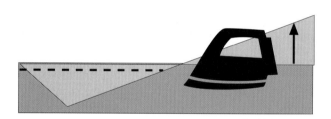

2. Press from the right side of the fabric. Move the iron across the width of the strips (in the direction of the arrow).

All designs in this book are strip cut with the 4-angle and the points or lines of the Starmaker 8 Master Template.

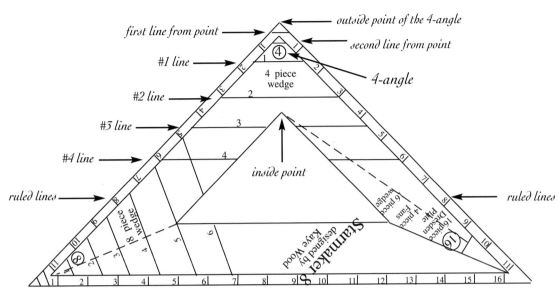

outside point of the 4-angle
second line from point
first line from point
#1 line
#2 line
#3 line
#4 line
ruled lines
4-angle
4 piece wedge
inside point
ruled lines
8 piece wedge
6 piece wedge
4 piece Dresden Fans
16 piece Dresden Plate
Starmaker 8 designed by Kaye Wood

These points and lines on the Starmaker 8 Master Template ensure accurate angles.

Strip cutting shapes with the 4-angle of the Starmaker 8
Look at all the possible shapes.

You may have already used several of these shapes in quilts, but now they are easier to cut.
The strips can be any width or can even be several strips sewn together into a combination strip.

The height of the shape is determined by the width of the strip or combination strip.

To cut these shapes:
1. Place the 4-angle of the Starmaker 8 with the point, or one of the lines, at the top of a strip of fabric.
2. Cut the shape shown.

1. Place the Starmaker 8
2. Cut the shape

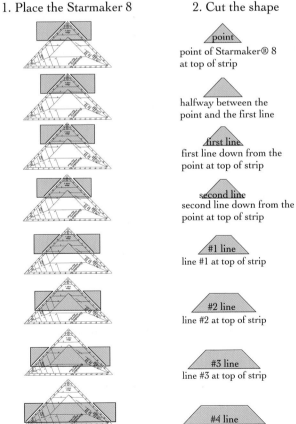

point
point of Starmaker® 8 at top of strip

halfway between the point and the first line

first line
first line down from the point at top of strip

second line
second line down from the point at top of strip

#1 line
line #1 at top of strip

#2 line
line #2 at top of strip

#3 line
line #3 at top of strip

#4 line
line #4 at top of strip

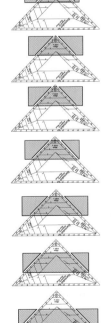

Chapter 1

Horizontal Triangles

Celebration Banner, made by Kaye Wood. Directions on page 20.

 Kaye Wood's Strip-Cut Quilts

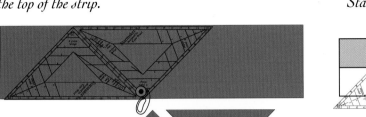

Two different triangles are cut from each strip or combination strip. The size of the triangle is determined by the width (height) of the combination strip.

Triangle A
Cut with the point of the 4-angle of the Starmaker 8 at the top of the strip.

Triangle B
Cut with the point of the 4-angle of the Starmaker 8 at the bottom of the strip.

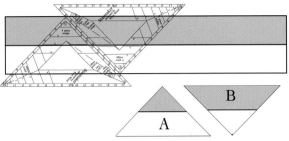

Strips can be one solid fabric, a stripe, or several strips sewn into a combination strip.

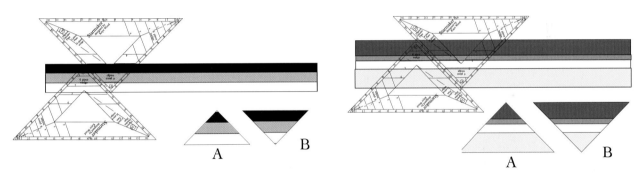

Strips can be all the same width, as shown above, or the combination strip can be made up of several different width strips.

To plan your own project, you need to know this information

How much fabric do I need?

Number of triangles in my quilt?_____
Select the width of strip (height of triangle)
The chart will give you number of triangles per strip.
For example, for 30 triangles with a strip width of 6 inches, you will need five strips.

five strips x 6 inches per strip = 30 inches of fabric

Strip-Cut Triangles

Combination strip width	Number of triangles per 44-inch strip
3 inches	13*
4 inches	9*
5 inches	7*
6 inches	6
7 inches	5*
7 3/4 inches	4
8 1/2 inches	4

*When cutting an uneven number of triangles, cut the second strip beginning with the triangle you have the least of.

Accurate Cutting

It is important to keep the Starmaker 8 straight on the fabric. Here are some guidelines to help you do that:

◆ Keep the horizontal lines on the Starmaker 8 parallel to the seamlines and to the edge of the strips.

◆ If one of the lines on the Starmaker 8 are exactly on the seamlines, use the line as a guide.

◆ If a line is not on the seamline, place a piece of Static Sticker or tape on the Starmaker 8 even with the bottom of the strip or on a seamline as a guide as you continue to cut triangles.

◆ Both sides of the bottom of the combination strip should end at the same marks on the ruled lines on the sides of the Starmaker 8. See page 9.

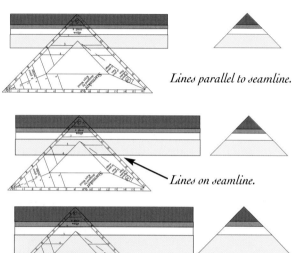

Lines parallel to seamline.

Lines on seamline.

Static Sticker at bottom.

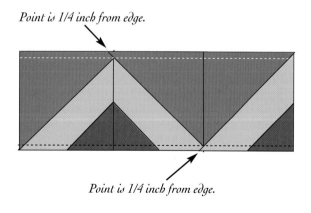

Point is 1/4 inch from edge.

Point is 1/4 inch from edge.

Matching Points

◆ Use 1/4-inch seam allowances.

◆ Match seamlines when necessary.

◆ Press accurately. See page 8.

◆ When sewing two blocks together, with diagonal seams coming together, the seams come to a "V" at 1/4 inch from the edge. This 1/4 inch is needed for the seam allowance when blocks or rows are sewn together.

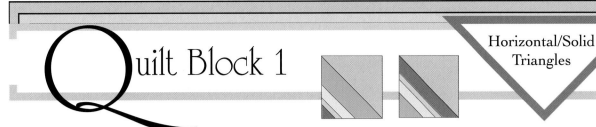

Quilt Block 1

1. **Make combination strips.**

   Sew two or more strips, right sides together, into a combination strip. Press seam allowances all in the same direction. See page 8.

2. **Cut solid strips.**

   Measure the width of the combination strip. Cut the solid fabric the same width.

3. **Sew tubes.**

   Sew the combination strip and the solid strip, right sides together, along both long edges so it forms a tube.

4. **Cut triangles.**

   Cut with the combination strip on top; keep the seamlines parallel to the lines on the Starmaker 8. See page 11.
   "A" triangles—cut with the point of the 4-angle of the Starmaker 8 at the top of the strip.
   "B" triangles—cut with the Starmaker 8 upside-down and the point of the 4-angle at the bottom of the strip.
   Remove two or three stitches at each point. Press seam allowances toward the solid strip. See page 8.

5. **Square up your blocks, if necessary.**

   If the blocks are not all the same size, square them up.
   Follow the directions on page 88.

6. **Lay out the design.**

   There are several possibilities, including those shown on the following pages. This quilt block is also great for border strips.

   Tubes make the triangles easier,
   but for accuracy sake, only use tubes
   when a solid strip is joined to a combination strip.

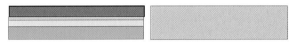

Cut the solid strip the same width as the combination strip.

Tube-sewing
It saves fabric, and you get two different quilt blocks. Strips can be solid, a stripe, or several strips sewn into a combination strip.

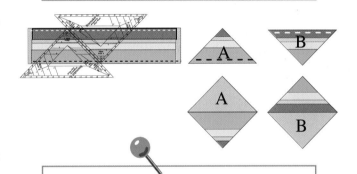

The solid fabric triangle is a great place to show off your quilting, your machine embroidery, or as an area to write names for a memory quilt.

The size of the block is determined by the width of the combination strip.

Yardages and sizes for Quilt Block 1 are on page 88.

Rainbow Sherbet

Finished size: 35-by-35 inches
A photo of this table cover or wallhanging,
by Kathleen Quinlan, is on the title page.

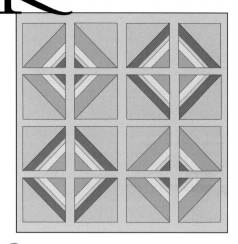

Are you pointless?

If you would rather not match seamlines and points, this design is for you!

Tip

If your combination strip is not 6 inches wide, cut the solid strips the width of your strip.

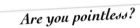

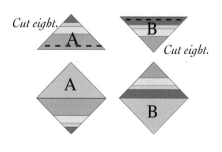

Cut eight.

A

B

Cut eight.

A

B

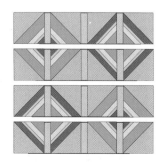

Fabric Requirements for Sixteen Blocks

Combination strips

Purple	1/4 yard	Cut three 2-by-44-inch strips.
Blue	1/8 yard	Cut three 1-by-44-inch strips.
Yellow	1/4 yard	Cut three 1 1/2-by-44-inch strips.
Green	1/3 yard	Cut three 3-by-44-inch strips.
Solid strips	1/2 yard	Cut three 6-by-44-inch strips.
Sashing	1 yard	
Backing and sleeve	1 yard	
Binding	1/3 yard	
Batting	37-by-37 inches	

1. **Make combination strips.**
   Sew the four strips, right sides together, into three combination strips. Follow the directions for Quilt Block 1 on page 13.
   Cut three solid strips 6 inches wide (the width of the combination strip).

2. **Tube-sew strips.**
   Sew the solid strips to the combination strips, following the directions for Quilt Block 1 on page 13.

3. **Cut triangles.**
   Cut eight "A" and eight "B" quilt blocks. See page 13.
   Square up the blocks if necessary. See page 88.

4. **Lay out the design.**
   There are several possibilities, including the one above and those shown on the next page.

5. **Make short sashing strips.**
   See page 89 for instructions. Cut twelve sashing strips 2-by-8 inches (or the size of the block).

6. **Sew into rows.**
   Alternate four blocks and three short sashing strips.

7. Make long sashing/border strips.

Cut seven sashing strips 2 inches wide. Pin-mark the strips (see page 89) to match seamlines.

8. Layer, quilt, and bind.

See page 92. For a wallhanging, add a sleeve before adding the binding.

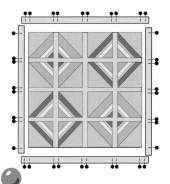

Great scrap quilts

The strips can be cut any size. Each set of triangles can be made from completely different fabric.

Try these designs.

Each one is made from eight "A" blocks and eight "B" blocks.
Experiment with different colors for the sashing and borders.

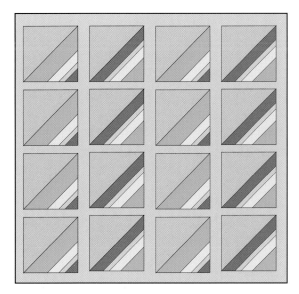

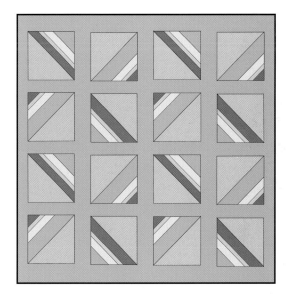

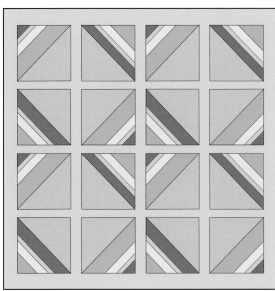

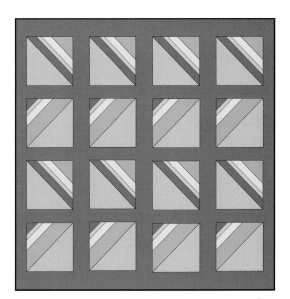

Quilt Block 2

Every strip can be the same width, or each strip can be a different width.

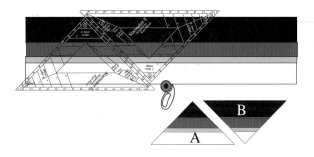

Sew "A" and "B" triangles together.

1. Make combination strips.

Sew two or more strips, right sides together, into a combination strip.

Press seam allowances all in the same direction. See page 8.

2. Cut triangles.

Cut "A" triangles with the point of the 4-angle of the Starmaker 8 at the top of the strip.

Cut "B" triangles with the Starmaker upside-down; the point of the 4-angle at the bottom of the strip.

3. Sew quilt blocks.

Sew one "A" and one "B" triangle, right sides together.

Press the seam allowance toward the darker fabric.

4. Square up the blocks, if necessary.

See page 88.

5. Lay out your design.

There are several possibilities, including those shown on the following pages. These blocks can also be used for border strips.

Yardages and sizes for Quilt Block 2 are on page 88.

Tablerunner Trio

Finished size: 22-by-42 inches
Photos of these quilts, made by Lori Jonsson,
are on the Table of Contents page (left edge).

Fabric Requirements for Each Quilt

Combination strips:

Black	1/3 yard	Cut three 3-by-44-inch strips.
Med. teal	1/8 yard	Cut three 1-by-44-inch strips.
Light teal	1/4 yard	Cut three 1 1/2-by-44-inch strips.
White	1/4 yard	Cut three 2-by-44-inch strips.

Sashing/borders 1/3 yard
Backing and sleeve 1 yard
Binding 1/3 yard
Batting (optional) 24-by-44 inches

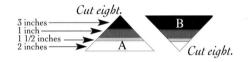

Another pointless design!
Have fun with these deigns.
They are great beginner projects.

1. ## Make combination strips.
   Sew the strips, right sides together, into three combination strips, as shown. Press seam allowances toward the black strip. See page 8.

2. ## Cut and sew triangles.
   Instructions for Quilt Block 2 are on page 16.
   Cut eight "A" and eight "B" triangles.
   Sew eight "A" and "B" triangles together.

Cut eight.

3 inches
1 inch
1 1/2 inches
2 inches

B

A

Cut eight.

Sew eight.

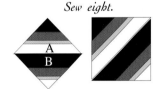

3. ## Make short sashing strips.
   Cut six sashing strips 2-by-8 inches (or size of block). See page 89.

4. ## Sew into rows.
   Sew two rows alternating blocks and sashing, following one of the above designs.

5. ## Make long sashing strips and borders.
   Cut four strips 2-by-44 inches. Cut one of these strips in half to use for the top and bottom border.
   Pin-mark and sew the long sashing/border strips to match seamlines. See page 89.
   Pin-mark and sew the top and bottom border strips.

6. ## Layer, quilt, and bind.
   See page 92.
   For a wallhanging, add a sleeve before adding the binding.

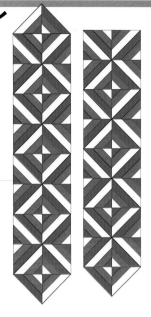

Christmas Tablerunners and Wallhangings

Finished size: 12 1/2-by-62 inches
A photo of the tablerunner, by Kaye Wood,
is on the Table of Contents page (lower right).

Fabric Requirements

Combination strips:

White	1/2 yard	Cut six 2-by-44-inch strips.
Red	1/2 yard	Cut six 2-by-44-inch strips.
Green	1/2 yard	Cut six 2-by-44-inch strips.
Backing	3/4 yard	Cut two 13-by-44-inch pieces.
Batting (optional)		14-by-64 inches

1. Make combination strips.

Sew 2-inch strips, right sides together, into six combination strips. Press seam allowances all in the same direction. See page 8.

2. Cut triangles.

Follow the cutting directions on page 16. Tablerunner: Cut eighteen "A" triangles and eighteen "B" triangles. Wallhanging: Cut seventeen "A" triangles and seventeen "B" triangles.

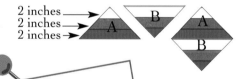

2 inches
2 inches
2 inches

3. Sew quilt blocks.

Follow instructions on page 16 for Quilt Block 2. Sew sixteen "A" and "B" triangles together to make sixteen blocks. Tablerunner: Two "A" and two "B" blocks are used on the ends. Wallhanging: One "A" and one "B" block is used on one end.

4. Sew into rows.

Sew blocks into two rows, each with eight blocks and one or two single triangles. Match seamlines. Press seam allowances.

5. Finish.

Tablerunner: Use an envelope finish and no batting. Wallhanging: Layer, quilt, add a sleeve at the top, and bind. See page 92.

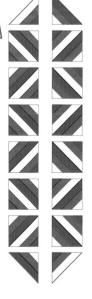

Merry Christmas!
Your Christmas table will look so festive. Be sure to make several of these for gifts. Try other seasonal colors!

Reflections

Fabric Requirements

Combination strips:

White	2/3 yard	Cut ten 2-by-44-inch strips.
Blue	2/3 yard	Cut ten 2-by-44-inch strips.
Black	2/3 yard	Cut ten 2-by-44-inch strips.
Borders	2/3 yard	Cut 3-by-44-inch strips.
Backing	46-by-70 inches	
Batting	46-by-70 inches	
Binding	1/3 yard	

1. ## Make combination strips.
   Sew 2-inch strips, right sides together, into ten combination strips.

2. ## Cut triangles.
   Cut sixty "A" and sixty "B" triangles, following the triangle cutting directions for Quilt Block 2 on page 16.

3. ## Sew blocks.
   Sew sixty "AB" blocks, following directions for Quilt Block 2, on page 16.

4. ## Sew into rows.
   Sew ten identical rows, matching seamlines.
   Turn every other row upside-down.
   Press seam allowances in opposite directions.

5. ## Finish.
   Add mitered or square borders, see pages 90 and 91.
   Cut six 3-inch strips. Pin-mark (see page 89) to match seamlines.
   Press seam allowances toward the border strip.
   Layer, quilt, and bind. See page 92.

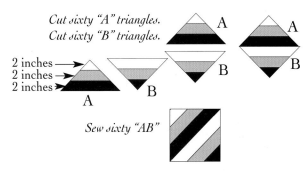

Cut sixty "A" triangles.
Cut sixty "B" triangles.

2 inches
2 inches
2 inches

A B A B A B

Sew sixty "AB"

Celebration Banner

(It's reversible!)

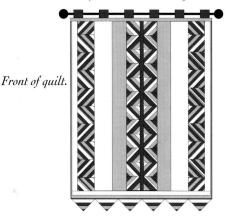

Front of quilt.

Back of quilt.

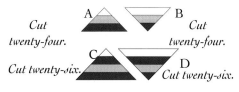

Reversible quilts are easy!
Both the front and back are joined and quilted at the same time. Get your serger out to save time. If not, just follow the instructions for sewing on a sewing machine.

A B
Cut
twenty-four.   Cut
twenty-four.
C
Cut twenty-six.   D
Cut twenty-six.

"C" and "D" triangles are larger than "A" and "B" triangles.

Sew twenty-four "AB."   Sew twenty "CD."

Fabric Requirements

White	2 yards
Light blue	2 yards
Dark blue	1-1/2 yards
Black	1/2 yard
Batting	60-by-50 inches

1. Cut strips.

Cut the 50-inch long strips lengthwise; cut the 44-inch long strips crosswise or lengthwise. (If necessary, two crosswise strips can be sewn together to get the 50-inch length.)

White — Cut four 5 1/2-by-50-inch strips, two 2-by-50-inch strips, and nine 2-by-44-inch strips.

Light blue — Cut four 4 1/2-by-50-inch strips, two 5 1/2-by-50-inch strips, and ten 2-by-44-inch strips.

Dark blue — Cut one 2-by-50-inch strip, two 4 1/2-by-50-inch strips, and fourteen 2-by-44-inch strips.

Black — Cut four 2-by-50-inch strips.

Batting — Cut three 2-by-50-inch strips, four 4 1/2-by-50-inch strips, and four 5-by-50-inch strips.

2. Make combination strips.

Sew four combination strips—2-by-44-inch strips of white/light blue/dark blue—for the "AB" triangles. Sew four combination strips—2-by-44-inch strips of white/dark blue/light blue/dark blue—for "CD" triangles. Press seam allowances all in the same direction. See page 8 for pressing instructions.

3. Cut triangles.

Cutting instructions are on page 16. Cut twenty-four "A" and twenty-four "B" triangles. Cut twenty-six "C" and twenty-six "D" triangles.

4. Sew quilt blocks.

Sew twenty-four "AB" blocks. See page 16 for Quilt Block 2. Sew only twenty "CD" blocks.

Tip

The rest of the "C" and "D" triangles will be used for the pointed edge at the bottom of the quilt.

5. Sew the triangles into vertical rows.

Sew two rows of twelve "AB" blocks.

Sew two rows of ten "CD" blocks.

6. Sew the rows together.

This quilt is reversible, and both front, back and the quilting are all done at the same time.

a. Start with the 2-inch center strip (right in the middle of the quilt). Make a sandwich with the 2-inch batting strip in the middle, the 2-inch fabric strips right side out. Serge or zigzag (down both long sides).

b. Add the next row in this manner:
Put the back strip right sides to the center back; Put the front strip right sides to the center front. Put a strip of batting underneath. Serge or straight-stitch all the layers together along one edge.

c. Open out the strips and batting.
The batting will be in the middle.
Serge or zigzag the long outside edge.

d. Repeat Steps b and c to continue adding rows.

7. Square up the quilt.

After all the rows are added, trim the top and bottom of the rows.

8. Sew bottom border strip.

Sew a 2-inch border strip to the bottom of the quilt, adding the back, front, and batting in the same way as the strips were added.

But do <u>not</u> serge or zigzag the outside edges closed.

9. Sew the bottom triangle edging.

Sew six triangles by sewing a "C" and a "D" triangle, right sides together with a triangle of batting underneath.

Sew along the two side edges, leaving the bottom open.

Turn the triangles right sides out (the batting will be in the middle).

Space, pin and sew the triangles right sides together to the bottom of just the front border strip.

Turn under the edge of the back border strip and hand-blindstitch or machine-topstitch the back border to the triangles.

10. Finish.

Cut the light blue into 3-inch binding strips.
Hanging tabs are on page 92.
Sew a binding on the two sides and top of the quilt, following instructions on page 92.

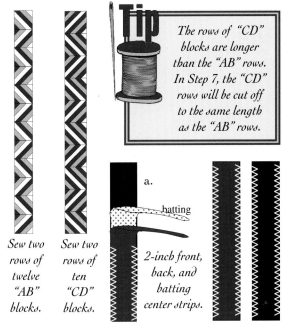

Tip

The rows of "CD" blocks are longer than the "AB" rows. In Step 7, the "CD" rows will be cut off to the same length as the "AB" rows.

Sew two rows of twelve "AB" blocks.

Sew two rows of ten "CD" blocks.

a.

batting

2-inch front, back, and batting center strips.

front   back

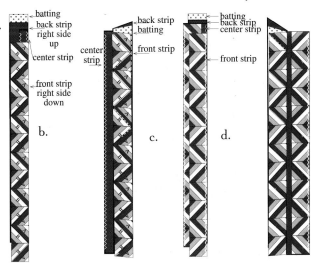

batting
back strip right side up
center strip
front strip right side down

b.

back strip
batting
center strip
front strip

c.

batting
back strip
center strip
front strip

d.

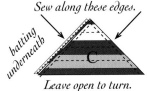

Tip

Check to see that serging stitches don't show on the right side. If stitching does show, just serge or straight-stitch a deeper seam.

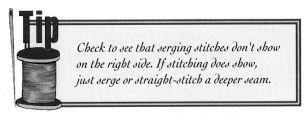

Sew along these edges.

batting underneath

C

Leave open to turn.

Front of quilt.

Back of quilt.

Random triangles

This is great for that scrap quilt look! Each triangle could be made from different fabrics. Just sew a bunch of strips together and cut triangles. Sew them together and see what you get. It's lots of fun!

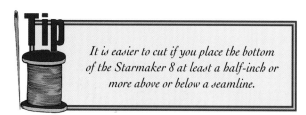

Tip

It is easier to cut if you place the bottom of the Starmaker 8 at least a half-inch or more above or below a seamline.

Randomly cut strips add excitement and movement to our quilts. Each triangle can be cut from a different section of the combination strip for a true scrap-looking quilt.

1. **Make combination strips.**
   Individual strips can be cut from 3/4 inch up to 3 inches wide. Cut and sew different width strips together into a combination strip that is at least 9 or 10 inches high.
   Press seam allowances toward the darker fabric. See pressing instructions, page 8.

2. **Cut triangles.**
   Cut triangles by placing the Starmaker 8 anywhere on the combination strip.
   The Starmaker 8 can be placed with the 4-angle even with the top or even with the bottom of the strip or anywhere on the combination strip. Triangles will be 8 1/2 inches high (the height of the Starmaker 8).

3. **Sew quilt blocks.**
   Sew any two triangles together to make a quilt block.
   Press seam allowances toward the darker fabric. See page 8.

4. **Square up the quilt blocks, if necessary.**
   See page 88.

5. **Lay out the design.**
   There are several possibilities, since every triangle can be different depending on where the Starmaker 8 was placed on the combination strip.

   These randomly cut quilt blocks can be used in many of the designs in this book. The triangles can also be combined with solid triangles, with vertical triangles, or with fussy-cut triangles.

Yardages and sizes for Quilt Block 3 are on page 88.

Scrap Happy

Finished size: 70-by-74 inches
A photo of this quilt, made by Joyce Horn,
is on the Table of Contents page (upper right).

Make this any size from a lap robe, a couch
throw, or a king-size bed.

Fabric Requirements

Combination strips (lots of scraps):
Solid strips   6-by-80 inches
   Brown   1 yard   Cut six 6-by-44-inch strips.
   Beige   1 yard   Cut four 6-by-80-inch strips.
Backing   75-by-80 inches
Batting   75-by-80 inches
Binding   3/4 yard   Cut eight 3-by-44-inch strips.

1. Make combination strips.
  Cut strips from scraps. Strips can be any
  width.
  See page 22.

2. Cut triangles.
  Cut a total of sixty-four triangles following
  directions for Quilt Block 3 on page 22.
  Triangles cut from the combination strip will
  be 8 1/2 inches high (the height of the
  Starmaker 8).

Cut sixty-four triangles.

3. Sew the triangles into blocks.
  Sew two triangles together to make thirty-two
  quilt blocks, following directions on page 22.

Sew thirty-two blocks.

4. Sew the blocks into rows.
  Each of the four rows has seven blocks.
  Press the seam allowances

Sew four rows.

5. Add long solid strips between block
  rows.
  Sew two 6-by-44-inch strips together to make
  each strip long enough. Pin-mark these strips.
  See page 89.

6. Layer, quilt, and bind.
  Cut eight 3-inch-wide binding strips.
  See instructions on page 92.

Another pointless design
This quilt is pointless and made of
scraps of solid strips between rows,
so no seams to match.
Have lots of fun with this one!

Quilt Block 4

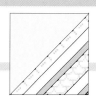

Scrap lovers:

*This quilt block is for you!
Use up some of your scraps and turn
them into a treasured quilt.*

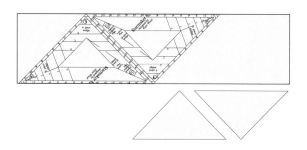

1. **Cut solid triangles.**
   Cut strips 8 1/2 inches high.
   Place the point of the 4-angle of the Starmaker 8 at the top of the strip. Cut on both sides of the Starmaker 8.
   Cut the second triangle by turning the Starmaker 8 upside-down and placing the point of the 4-angle of the Starmaker 8 at the bottom of the strip.

2. **Make scrap triangles.**
   Cut strips 1 1/2 to 2 1/2 inches wide from your scraps.
   Cut one of these strips 19-inch-long strip for the bottom of a triangle; this is the longest strip needed.
   Sew a strip to one side of the 19-inch strip by sewing the strips right sides together. Press the seams toward the bottom strip.
   Trim the length of these strips by placing the Starmaker 8 on the bottom of the 19-inch strip and cutting along the shape of the Starmaker 8.
   Add more strips and trim the ends by placing the Starmaker 8 at the bottom of the long strip. Continue adding strips and trimming the sides until the triangle is complete.

3. **Sew triangles together.**
   Sew a solid triangle and a scrap triangle together to make a quilt block.
   Press seam allowances toward the solid triangle.

4. **Square up quilt blocks, if necessary.**
   See page 88.

5. **Lay out the design.**
   These quilt blocks can fit into any of the designs used in this book that are made from a solid/pieced triangle.

*Yardages and sizes for Quilt Block 4
are on page 88.*

Kaye Wood's Strip-Cut Quilts

Rosebud Baby Quilt

Finished size: 32-by-45 inches
A photo of this quilt, made by Kaye Wood, is on page 6.

Fabric Requirements

Strips (lots of scraps)   Need six 8 1/2-inch triangles.
Solid strips   1/2 yard Cut two 8 1/2-by-44-inch strips.
Sashing/borders 2/3 yard Cut five 3 1/2-by-44-inch strips.
Backing   35-by-48 inches
Batting   35-by-48 inches
Gathered eyelet 175 inches

1. ### Create triangles.
   Sew strips together to make six 8 1/2-inch-high scrap triangles.
   Cut six triangles from the 8 1/2-inch-wide solid strips.
   See page 24.

2. ### Put together quilt blocks.
   Make six quilt blocks, following directions for Quilt Block 4 on page 24.

3. ### Make short sashing strips.
   Cut four 3 1/2-by-11 1/2-inch strips .
   Follow directions on page 89.
   Sew into two rows each with three blocks.

4. ### Make long sashing strip.
   Cut one 3 1/2-inch strip.
   Pin-mark the strip. See page 89.

5. ### Finish.
   For the borders, pin-mark the top and bottom border strips. See page 89. Pin-mark the side border strips.
   To do the eyelet edging, see page 91.
   Do an envelope finish. See page 91.
   Machine tie as shown on page 92.

Chapter 2

Spool Quilts

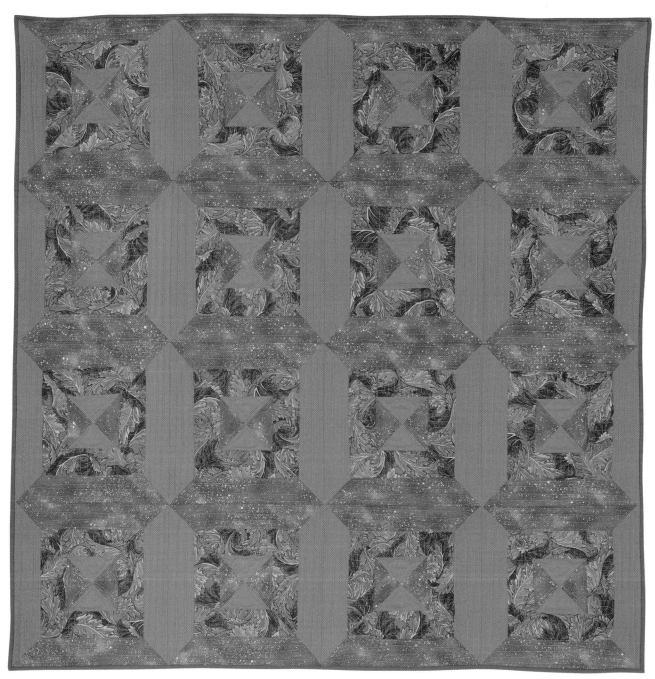

Emeralds and Amethysts, made by Kathleen Quinlan. Directions on page 31.

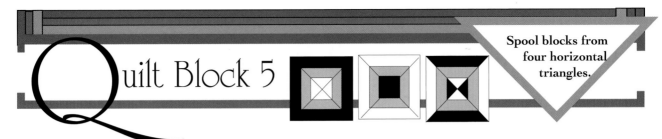

Quilt Block 5

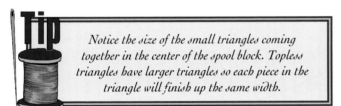

Try the three blocks above for practice projects.

1. **Make combination strips.**
   Cut and sew three strips of fabric, right sides together into a combination strip.
   Press seam allowances toward the darker fabric. See pressing instructions, page 8.

2. **Cut triangles.**
   Cut "A" and "B" triangles (see page 11), or cut "A" and "B" triangles (see page 28).

Experiment with triangles—
Try both triangles and topless triangles.
Choose which you prefer and continue with one or more of the quilts on the following pages.

Practice blocks make great potholders!

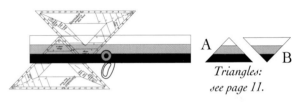

Triangles: see page 11.

Topless triangles: see page 28.

Tip
Notice the size of the small triangles coming together in the center of the spool block. Topless triangles have larger triangles so each piece in the triangle will finish up the same width.

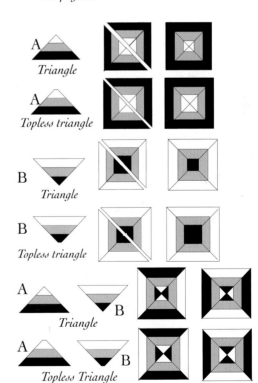

Triangle

Topless triangle

Triangle

Topless triangle

Triangle

Topless Triangle

3. **Sew the quilt block.**
   Sew four triangles or four topless triangles together to make one or more of these spool designs.

   Sew two triangles, matching seamlines, together to make half of each quilt block.
   Press seam allowances on each half in opposite directions.

   Sew two halves together, matching seamlines, to make the quilt block.
   Press seam allowances.

4. **Square up the blocks, if necessary.**
   See page 88.

Topless triangles will be slightly larger so the quilted project will be a little larger than the sizes listed. Fabric amounts listed will be enough for either cutting method.

Yardages and sizes for Quilt Block 5 are on page 88.

Topless Triangles

Use only when it is important for each piece in the triangle to finish the same width.

Triangle A

Cut with the top of the strip halfway between the point of the 4-angle *and* the first line on the Starmaker 8.

Triangle B

Cut with the bottom of the strip halfway between the point of the 4-angle *and* the first line on the Starmaker 8.

Do not confuse the #1 line on the Starmaker 8 with the first line from the point. See page 9.

Topless triangles are sometimes used for spool quilt blocks and for designs like this.

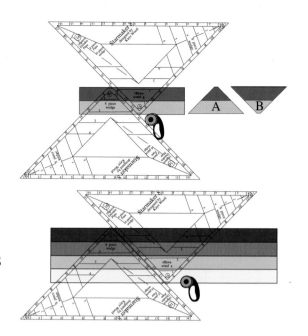

Topless triangles.
The points at the top of the triangle are cut off.

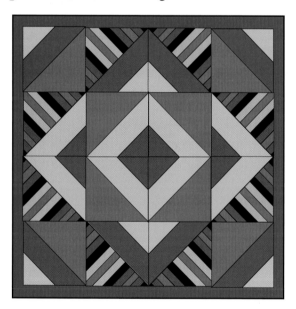

The size of the small pieces (solid brown and light green) in each triangle look best if they finish the same width as the other pieces in the triangle.

The advantage of using topless triangles is that each piece in the triangle finishes the same width.

If you cut triangles, with the point of the Starmaker 8 at the top or bottom of the strip, the small piece will be narrower than the rest of the pieces, which is okay for some designs.

Which cutting method?
Each project will specify whether to cut triangles or topless triangles. Some projects can use either, depending on the finished look you want.

Topless Triangles

combination strip width	number of triangles per 44-inch strip
2 1/2 inches	14
3 inches	13*
4 inches	8
5 inches	6
6 inches	5*
7 inches	4
7 3/4 inches	4
8 1/2 inches	3*

*When cutting an uneven number of triangles, cut the second strip beginning with the triangle you have the least of.

Two Fun Spool Quilts

(Instructions on this page and the next)

Finished size of both quilts: 47-by-74 inches

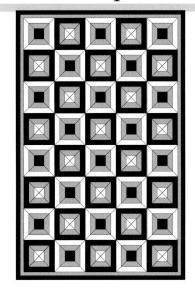

Fabric Requirements

Combination strips:
  White 1 3/4 yard Cut twenty-seven 2-by-44-inch strips.
  Blue 1 3/4 yard Cut twenty-seven 2-by-44-inch strips.
  Black 1 3/4 yard Cut twenty-seven 2-by-44-inch strips.
First border 1/2 yard Cut eight 2-by-44-inch strips.
Second border 1 yard Cut eight 3-by-44-inch strips.
Backing 50-by-78 inches
Batting 50-by-78 inches
Binding 1/2 yard

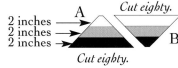
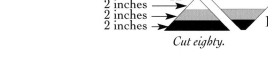

2 inches → A   Cut eighty.
2 inches →
2 inches →   B
Cut eighty.

1. ## Make combination strips.
   Sew 2-inch strips, right sides together, into twenty-seven combination strips.

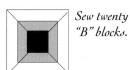

Sew twenty "A" blocks.   Sew twenty "B" blocks.

2. ## Cut triangles.
   Cut eighty "A" and eighty "B" topless triangles, following the directions on page 28.

3. ## Sew the triangles into blocks.
   Sew twenty "A" blocks and twenty "B" blocks, following the direction for Quilt Block 5, page 27.

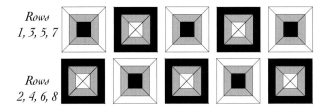

Rows 1, 3, 5, 7

Rows 2, 4, 6, 8

4. ## Sew the blocks into rows.
   Alternate blocks, matching seamlines. Press the seam allowances for each row in opposite directions.

5. ## Sew the rows together.
   Match seamlines.
   Press seam allowances.

6. ## Finish.
   Add borders. See page 90.
     Cut eight 2-inch and eight 3-inch border strips, see above.
     Pin-mark the center and both ends of the border strips. See page 89.
   Press seam allowances toward the border strip.
   Layer, quilt, and bind. See page 92.

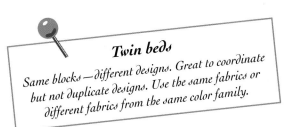

Twin beds
Same blocks—different designs. Great to coordinate but not duplicate designs. Use the same fabrics or different fabrics from the same color family.

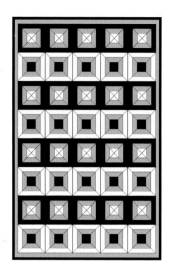

Fabric Requirements

Combination strips:
White 1 3/4 yard Cut twenty-seven 2-by-44-inch strips.
Blue   1 3/4 yard Cut twenty-seven 2-by-44-inch strips.
Black 1 3/4 yard Cut twenty-seven 2-by-44-inch strips.
First border
            1/2 yard   Cut eight 2-by-44-inch strips.
Second border
            1 yard   Cut eight 3-by-44-inch strips.
Backing 50-by-78 inches
Batting 50-by-78 inches
Binding 1/2 yard

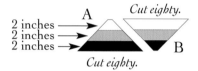

A   Cut eighty.

2 inches →
2 inches →
2 inches →

Cut eighty.   B

Sew twenty "A" blocks.

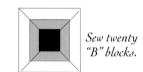

Sew twenty "B" blocks.

1. **Make combination strips.**
   Sew 2-inch strips, right sides together, into twenty-seven combination strips.

2. **Cut triangles.**
   Cut eighty "A" and eighty "B" topless triangles, following the directions on page 28.

3. **Sew the triangles into blocks.**
   Sew twenty "A" blocks and twenty "B" blocks, following the direction for Quilt Block 5, page 27.

4. **Sew the blocks into rows.**
   Sew into rows of the same blocks.
   Press the seam allowances for each row in opposite directions.

5. **Sew the rows together.**
   Matching seamlines.
   Press seam allowances.

6. **Finish.**
   Add borders. See page 90.
      Cut eight 2-inch and eight 3-inch border strips, see above.
      Pin-mark the center and both ends of the border strips. See page 89.

   Press seam allowances toward the border strip.
   Layer, quilt, and bind. See page 92.

Rows 1, 3, 5, 7

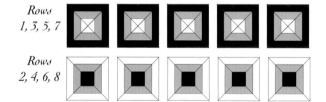

Rows 2, 4, 6, 8

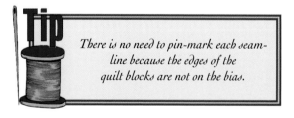

There is no need to pin-mark each seam-line because the edges of the quilt blocks are not on the bias.

Emeralds and Amethysts

Finished size: 35 1/2-by-35 1/2 inches
A photo of this quilt, made by Kathleen Quinlan, is on page 26.

Fabric Requirements

Combination strips:

Purple	1 yard	Cut eleven 2-by-44-inch strips.
Green	1 yard	Cut eleven 2-by-44-inch strips.
Lavender	1 yard	Cut eleven 2-by-44-inch strips.
Backing	1 1/2 yards	40-by-40 inches
Batting	40-by-40 inches	
Binding	1/4 yard	Cut four 1 3/4-inch strips.

1. **Make combination strips.**
   Sew the 2-inch strips, right sides together, into eleven combination strips.

2. **Cut triangles.**
   Cut thirty-two "A" and thirty-two "B" topless triangles.
   Follow directions on page 28.

3. **Sew the triangles into blocks.**
   Sew sixteen "AB" blocks, following directions for Quilt Block 5 on page 27.

4. **Sew into rows.**
   Sew the blocks into four identical rows, matching seamlines.
   Press the seamlines, alternating direction with every row.

5. **Sew the rows together, matching seamlines.**

6. **Finish.**
   Layer, quilt, and bind. See page 92.

Shades of color
Try two different shades of one color together with a coordinating print.

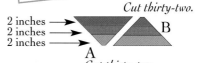

Cut thirty-two.

2 inches →
2 inches →
2 inches →

B

A

Cut thirty-two.

Sew sixteen "AB" blocks.

Spools of Lace

Finished size: 33-by-48 inches
A photo of this quilt, made by Kaye Wood,
is on page Kaye Wood welcome page (at front).

(Trimmed with lace!)

Fabric Requirements

Combination strips:

Blue	3/4 yard	Cut eight 3-inch strips.
Beige	1/2 yard	Cut eight 1 1/2-inch strips.
Green	1/2 yard	Cut eight 1 1/2-inch strips.
Print	3/4 yard	Cut eight 3-inch strips.
Lace	20 yards	(1-inch wide)
Sashing/Borders	1 yard	Cut eleven 3-inch strips.
Backing	40-by-55 inches	
Batting	40-by-55 inches	

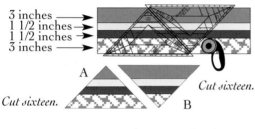

3 inches →
1 1/2 inches →
1 1/2 inches →
3 inches →

A

Cut sixteen.

B

Cut sixteen.

A   B

1. Make combination strips.

Sew four strips, right sides together, into eight combinations strips.

Press seam allowances. See page 8.

2. Cut triangles.

Cut sixteen "A" and sixteen "B" triangles. See page 8.

3. Add lace.

Sew flat or gathered lace, right sides together, to the bottom of each "A" and "B" triangle.

Press the seam allowances away from the lace and toward the triangles.

Trim the both ends of the lace with the Starmaker 8.

Sew eight "AB" blocks

4. Sew quilt blocks.

Sew the triangles into eight "AB" blocks. See page 27 for quilt block 5.

Sew all the way to the end of the lace.

Be sure to sew with the seam allowances away from the lace.

Measure the quilt block, including seam allowances.

Stitch-in-the-ditch

Ends of sashing strips are pressed under 1/4 inch.

Sashing strip lays under the quilt block and lace.

5. Short sashing strips.

Cut four short sashing strips 3 inches by the quilt block measurement.

Press under 1/4 inch on both ends of the sashing strips.

Sew short sashing strips to four quilt blocks.

Lay a quilt block on top of a sashing strip, both right sides up; line up one long raw edge of the sashing with the raw edge of the quilt block.

Pin the block to the sashing strip and stitch-in-the-ditch. (Sew on the seamline between the lace and the triangle.)

6. Sew into rows. Sew the blocks into four rows, each with two blocks and one sashing strip, following the directions in Step 6.

Measure the row, including the outside seam allowances.

7. Create sashing/borders.

Cut three sashing strips 3 inches by the row measurement. Press under 1/4 inch on both ends of the sashing strips.

Pin-mark these strips. See page 89.

Place the sashing strip under the row with the lace on top, both right sides up, with the raw edge of the sashing strip lined up with the raw edge of the quilt blocks.

Pin through the quilt blocks and the sashing strip. Stitch-in-the-ditch only on the seamline between the lace and quilt block.

Pin the folded end of the short sashing strips on top of the long sashing strips.

Sew one of these ways:

a. *The easy way* — Topstitch along the folded edge.

b. *A little more difficult* — Bring the raw edges of the short and long sashing strips, right sides together. Sew along the creased fold of the short sashing strip, from seamline to seamline.

Cut the top and bottom sashing strips 3-by-35 inches (to allow for mitered corners). Pin-mark. See page 89.

Sew to the top and bottom rows, using the same techniques above.

Cut four side border strips 3-by-44 inches. Sew two together to get the needed length — 3-by-55 inches.

Sew to quilt, using the same techniques above.

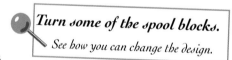
Turn some of the spool blocks. See how you can change the design.

8. Finish.

Miter the corners of the border strips. See page 91.

Sew lace, right sides together, to the outside edge of the quilt top.

Pin lace in towards the quilt top to keep it from being caught in the seams.

Use an envelope style finish. See page 91.

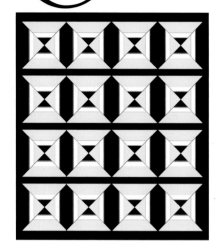

Glacier Ice

Fabric Requirements

Combination strips:

Black	1 2/3 yard	Cut sixteen 3-inch strips.
Light teal	1/2 yard	Cut sixteen 1-inch strips.
White	1 yard	Cut sixteen 2-inch strips.
Teal	2 yards	Cut sixteen 4-inch strips.
Sashing/borders	1 yard	Cut fourteen 2-inch strips.
Backing	70-by-75 inches	
Batting	70-by-75 inches	
Binding	1/2 yard	

Another pointless design

Triangles from different width strips — 3, 1, 2, and 4 inches — so when they go together, no seams will match. Sashing strips between rows, so no seams to match. Have lots of fun with this one!

3 inches
1 inch
2 inches
4 inches

A   B

Cut thirty-two of each "A" and "B".

1. Make combination strips.

Sew four strips, right sides together, into sixteen combination strips.

2. Cut triangles.

Cut thirty-two "A" and thirty-two "B" triangles, following directions on page 12.

Sew sixteen "AB" blocks.

3. Sew the triangles into blocks.

Sew the "A" and "B" triangles into sixteen blocks, following directions for Quilt Block 5 on page 27.

4. Sew the blocks into rows.

Sew four identical rows.
Press the seam allowances for each row in opposite directions.

5. Sashing strips.

Add long sashing strips between rows.
Cut fourteen sashing strips 2 inches wide.
Pin-mark the sashing strips. See page 89.

6. Finish quilt.

Pin-mark the center and both ends of the border strips. See page 89.
Add mitered or square borders. See pages 90 and 91.

Press seam allowances toward the border strip.
Layer, quilt, and bind. See page 92.

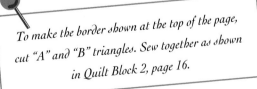

To make the border shown at the top of the page, cut "A" and "B" triangles. Sew together as shown in Quilt Block 2, page 16.

Chapter 3

Random Vertical Triangles

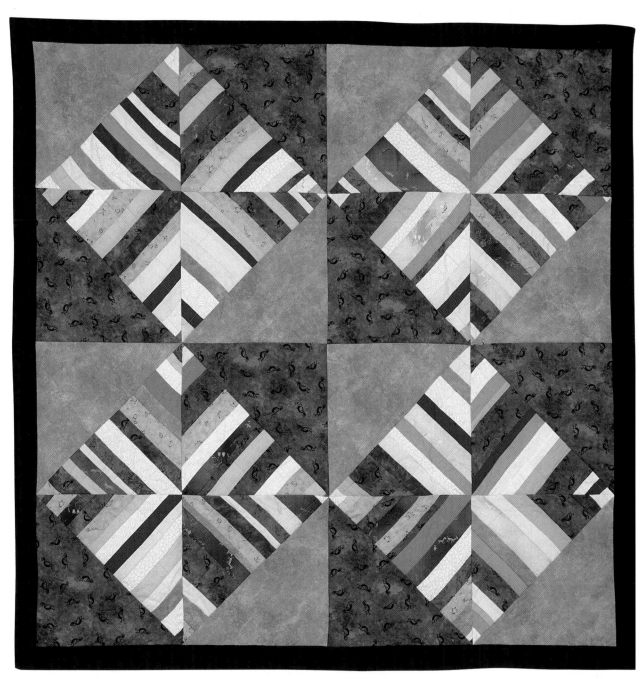

Ferris Wheel, made by Kaye Wood. Directions on page 38.

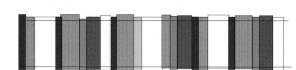

Random-Width Vertical Triangles

1. **Make combination strips.**

   Sew strips of fabrics, all the same height, together into a combination strip approximately 42 to 44 inches long. The height of the strips (from 3 to 9 inches) is determined by the project. See below.

   Press seam allowances all in one direction. Trim the bottom and top edges to straighten the strip.

2. **Cut triangles with the Starmaker 8.**

   Cut the first triangle with the point of the 4-angle of the Starmaker 8 at the top of the strip. Cut the next triangle with the point of the 4-angle of the Starmaker 8 at the bottom of the strip.

Another pointless design

No seams to match, so it's great for those pointless people. Use scraps of fabric or fat quarters, cut 9 inches long and random widths, from 1 to 4 inches.

Tip

To keep the Starmaker 8 straight, line up the outside and inside points on the same strip. See page 9 The horizontal lines and the bottom of the Starmaker 8 should be parallel to the top and bottom of the strip.

3 1/2-inch height

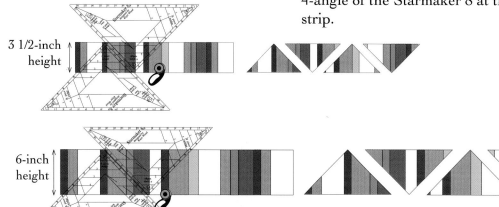

6-inch height

8 1/2-inch height

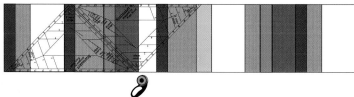

Quilt Block 6 *Quilt Block 7* *Quilt Block 8*

These triangles can be used in several different ways— joined with the same triangle into a quilt block, combined with solid triangles, or combined with horizontal strips. See the following pages.

Quilt Block 6

Random Vertical/ Solid Triangles

Tube-sewing makes the triangles easier to cut, but for accuracy sake, only use tubes when one of the strips is a solid piece of fabric, such as this design.

1. **Make vertical strips.**

   Cut a strip vertically or follow instructions for sewing vertical strips on page 36.

2. **Cut solid strips.**

   Measure the width of the vertical combination strip.
   Cut the solid fabric the same width.

3. **Tube-sew.**

   Sew the vertical combination strip and the solid strip, right sides together, along both long edges so it forms a tube.

4. **Cut triangles.**

   Cut the tube into triangles with the point of the 4-angle of the Starmaker 8 first at the top of the strip. Cut the next triangle by turning the Starmaker upside-down with the point of the 4-angle at the bottom of the strip.

   Remove two or three stitches at each point. Press seam allowances toward the solid strip.

5. **Square up blocks, if necessary.**

   See page 88.

6. **Lay out the design.**

   There are several possibilities, including those shown on the following pages.
   The designs are also great for border strips.

   Yardages and sizes for Quilt Block 6 are on page 88.

Get rid of some fat.

The random strips are perfect for all those fat quarters you've been collecting.

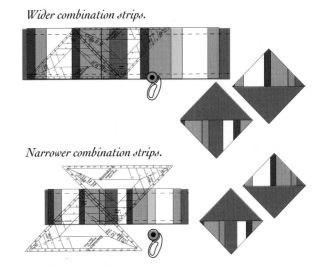

Wider combination strips.

Narrower combination strips.

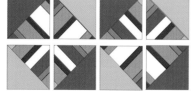

Ferris Wheel

Finished size: 47-by-47 inches
A photo of this quilt, made
by Kaye Wood, is on page 35.

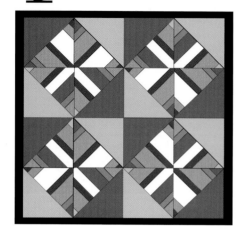

Fabric Requirements

Strips	Enough for four 9-by-44-inch strips.	
Solid triangles		
light	1/2 yard	Cut two 8 1/2-by-44-inch strips.
dark	1/2 yard	Cut two 8 1/2-by-44-inch strips.
Borders	1/2 yard	Cut eight 2-by-44-inch strips.
Backing/sleeve	2 1/2 yards	
Batting	50-by-50 inches	
Binding	1/3 yard	

1. Make vertical combination strips.
   Directions are on page 36.
   Cut strips 9 inches high by various widths from 1 to 3 inches.
   Sew these strips into four vertical combination strips 44 inches long.
   Trim the vertical strips to make the height 8 1/2 inches.

2. Sew tubes.
   Cut solid-colored strips the same width (8 1/2 inches).
   Follow directions for Quilt Block 6 on page 37.
   Sew two tubes with light-colored solid strip.
   Sew two tubes with the dark-colored solid strip.

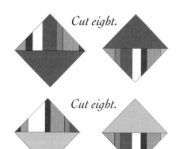

Cut eight.

Cut eight.

3. Cut triangles.
   Cut eight dark and eight light triangles using the Starmaker 8. Follow directions for Quilt Block 6 on page 37.

4. Sew the blocks into four rows.
   Match the diagonal seamlines.
   Press the seam allowances for each row in opposite directions.

5. Sew the rows together.
   Match the diagonal seamlines.
   Press seam allowances.

6. Finish.
   Add mitered or square borders. See pages 90 and 91.
      Cut eight 2-inch strips; sew two strips together for each border.
      Pin-mark to match seamlines. See page 89.
   Press seam allowances toward the border strip.
   Layer, quilt, and bind. See page 92.
   Add a sleeve if this is to be a wallhanging.
   See instructions on page 92.

Rows 1 and 3

Rows 2 and 4

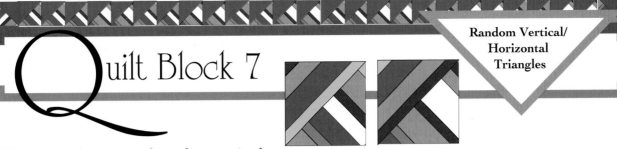

Quilt Block 7

Random Vertical/
Horizontal
Triangles

Either the horizontal or the vertical
strips, or both, may be cut randomly.

1. **Make horizontal combination strips.**
   Sew two or more strips together to make a
   horizontal combination strip.

2. **Cut horizontal triangles.**
   "A" triangles: Place the point of the 4-angle
   of the Starmaker 8 at the top of the strip.
   "B" triangles: Place the point of the 4-angle
   of the Starmaker 8 at the bottom of the strip.

3. **Make vertical combination strips.**
   Cut a stripe vertically or follow instructions
   for sewing vertical strips on page 36.
   Trim the vertical strip the same height as
   the horizontal strip.

4. **Cut vertical triangles.**
   Follow directions on page 36.

5. **Sew quilt block.**
   Sew each "A" and "B" horizontal triangle to a
   vertical triangle.
   Press seam allowances toward the horizontal
   triangle.
   Follow pressing instructions on page 8.

6. **Square up quilt blocks, if necessary.**
   See page 88.

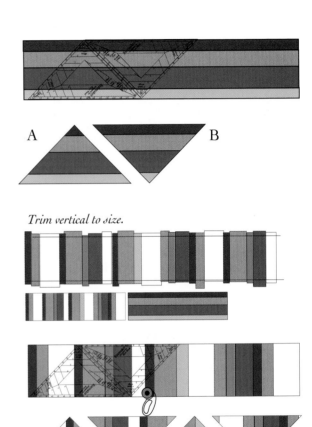

A   B

Trim vertical to size.

*Yardages and sizes for Quilt Block 7
are on page 88.*

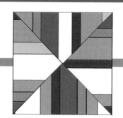

Quilt Block 8

Scrap Happy Pillow

Make it from this quilt block; see photo on page 87.

1. **Make vertical combination strips.**
   Cut a stripe vertically, or follow instructions for sewing vertical strips on page 39.

2. **Cut triangles.**
   Cut triangles with the point of the 4-angle of the Starmaker 8 first at the top of the strip. Cut the next triangle by turning the Starmaker upside-down with the point of the 4-angle at the bottom of the strip.

3. **Sew quilt block.**
   Sew two triangles, right sides together, to make each half of the quilt block.
   Press seam allowances in opposite directions.
   Sew two halves together, matching center seam-lines.
   Press seam allowances.

4. **Square up quilt blocks.**
   If necessary, see page 88.

5. **Lay out the design.**
   Play with the blocks until you have a pleasing design.

*Yardages and sizes for Quilt Block 8
are on page 88.*

Scraps, Scraps, and More Scraps

Fabric Requirements

Strips	Use assorted fabric scraps.
Border	1/2 yard Cut eight 2-by-44-inch strips.
Backing/sleeve	2 yards
Batting	55-by-55 inches
Binding	1/3 yard

1. Make combination strips.

Follow directions for cutting vertical strips on page 36.

Cut strips 9-inch-high by various widths from 1 to 3 inches.

Sew into nine combination strips 9-by-42 inches.

Trim these combination strips to 8 1/2 inches wide.

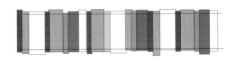

2. Cut triangles.

Cut thirty-six triangles using the Starmaker 8 and following instructions on page 40 for Quilt Block 8.

Cut thirty-six.

3. Sew quilt blocks.

Sew nine blocks, each made from four triangles.

Follow directions on page 40 for Quilt Block 8.

Sew nine.

4. Sew into rows.

Sew three quilt blocks each of three rows, matching seamlines.

Press seam allowances for each row in opposite directions.

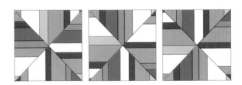

5. Finish.

Add mitered or square borders; see pages 90 and 91.

Cut eight 2-by-44-inch border strips.

Pin-mark to match seamlines. See page 89.

Press seam allowances toward the border strip.

Layer and quilt. See page 92.

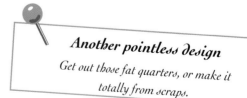

Another pointless design
Get out those fat quarters, or make it totally from scraps.

Chapter 4

Horizontal Fussy-Cut Triangles

Southwest Crossing, made by Lori Jonsson. Directions on page 45.

Large florals, stars, geometric shapes, or fabric scenes are all great for fussy-cuts.
The strips used for fussy-cuts can be any width.

With a strip or combination strip, the fabric motif is centered side-to-side in the middle of the Starmaker 8 with the point of the 4-angle of the Starmaker 8 at the top of the strip.

Some designs can also be used if they are cut upside-down, but this depends on your fabric motif pattern.

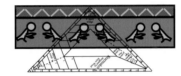

Motifs can also be centered by cutting with one of the lines (instead of the point) of the 4-angle on the Starmaker 8 at the top of the strip. Strips are then sewn to the top and or bottom of this motif shape and the triangle is cut using the Starmaker 8.

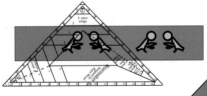

When a motif is randomly spaced on the fabric, place the point of the 4-angle of the Starmaker 8 above the motif, with the design centered side-to-side.

Fussy-cut triangles can be used completely in a quilt, or they may be combined with solid triangles, randomly cut horizontal, or vertical triangles for interesting quilt designs.
Try several designs on the following pages.

Quilt Block 9

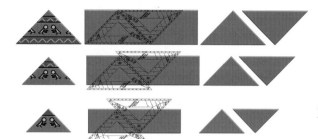

Tube-sewing

*It saves fabric, and you get two different quilt blocks.
Strips can be solid, a stripe, or several
strips sewn into a combination strip.*

1. Make horizontal fussy-cut triangles.
   The projects on the following pages will give
   strip or triangle sizes to cut.
   Follow directions on page 43.

2. Cut solid-colored strips.
   Measure the height of the horizontal fussy triangle.
   Cut the solid fabric the same width.
   Cut this strip into triangles, by placing the
   point of the 4-angle of the Starmaker 8 at the
   top of the strip; cut the next triangle by turning the Starmaker upside-down with the point
   of the 4-angle at the bottom of the strip.

3. Sew the quilt blocks.
   Sew a horizontal fussy-cut triangle, right sides
   together, to a solid triangle. Press seam
   allowances toward the darker fabric.

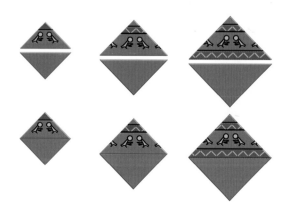

4. Square up blocks, if necessary.
   See page 88.

5. Lay out the design.
   There are several possibilities, including those
   shown on the following pages.
   These quilt blocks are also great for border
   strips.

*Yardages and sizes for Quilt Block 9
are on page 88.*

Southwest Crossing

Finished size: 26 1/2-by-26 1/2 inches
A photo of this quilt, made by
Lori Jonsson, is on page 42.

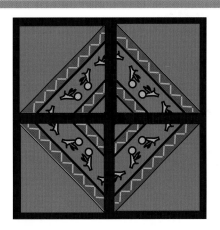

Fabric Requirements

Motif fabric	Enough for four 8 1/2-inch motifs.
Solid triangles	1/4 yard
Sashing/borders	1/2 yard
Backing/sleeve	1 yard
Batting	30-by-30 inches
Binding	1/4 yard

1. Make fussy-cut triangles.

Cut four triangles, with the motif centered, the same size as the Starmaker 8 (height of 8 1/2 inches).

For instructions, see page 43.

2. Cut solid triangles.

Cut one solid-colored strip 8 1/2-by-44 inches. Cut four triangles, following the cutting directions for Quilt Block 9 on page 44.

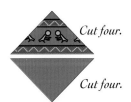

Cut four.

Cut four.

3. Sew quilt blocks.

Sew four quilt blocks, each made from a motif and a solid triangle.

Press the seam allowances toward the solid fabric.

Sew four.

4. Short sashing strips.

Cut two sashing strips 2-by-11 1/2 inches (or the size of your quilt block).

Sew two rows of two blocks with a short sashing strip in between, as shown. See page 89.

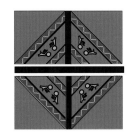

5. Long sashing strip.

Cut one sashing strip 2-by-30 inches.

Pin-mark to match seams. See page 89.

6. Finish.

Add mitered or square borders. See pages 90 and 91.

Cut four 2-inch strips. Pin-mark to match seamlines. See page 89.

Press seam allowances toward the border strip.

Layer, quilt, add sleeve, and bind. See page 92.

Chapter 5

Vertical Fussy-Cut Triangles

Painted Desert, made by Kaye Wood. Directions on page 50.

1. Make combination strips.

Choose an evenly striped fabric or sew together strips of fabric to make a striped combination.

Choose the "A" color strip you want in the very center of the triangle.
The "B" strips on either side of the center should be the same color and width. "C" strips should also be the same color and width, etc.

2. Cut triangles.

Cut triangles by centering the outside and inside points of the 4-angle of the Starmaker 8 on an "A" strip. See page 9.

Cut the next triangle by again centering the points of the Starmaker 8 on an "A" strip.

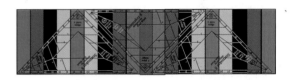

Second triangles: In-between the fussy-cut triangles, turn the Starmaker 8 upside-down to cut triangles with different color combinations. However, with careful strip placement, these second triangles can also have the same "A" strip centered in the triangle.

Second triangles.

Fussy-cut triangles can be used completely in a quilt,
or they may be combined with solid triangles,
randomly cut horizontal, or vertical triangles
for interesting quilt designs.
Try several designs on the following pages.

Quilt Block 10

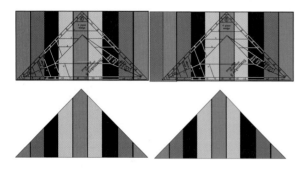

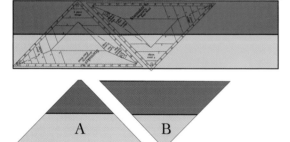

Triangles.

A   B

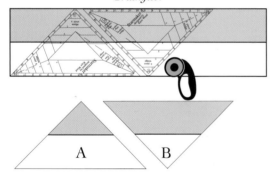

Topless triangles.

A   B

1. **Make vertical combination strip.**
   Choose a striped fabric or sew together strips of fabric to make a vertical combination strip.

2. **Cut vertical triangles.**
   See page 47.

3. **Make horizontal triangles.**
   Cut the horizontal triangles. See page 11.
   Or cut topless triangles. See page 28.
   Each project will suggest one or the other of these triangle methods.

4. **Sew the quilt blocks.**
   Sew one vertical and one horizontal triangle, right sides together, to make one block.
   Press seam allowances toward the horizontal stripped triangle.

5. **Square up the blocks, if necessary.**
   See page 88.

6. **Lay out the design.**
   There are several possibilities, including those shown on the following pages.
   The quilt blocks are also great for border strips.

Yardages and sizes for Quilt Block 10 are on page 88.

Quilt Block 11

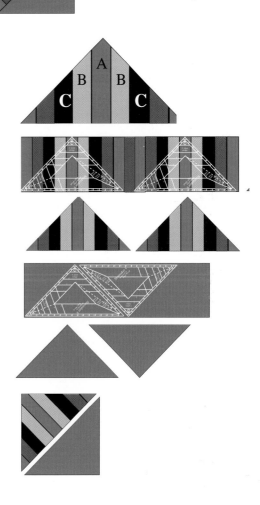

1. **Make vertical combination strip.**
   Choose a striped fabric or sew together strips of fabric to make a striped combination strip. See page 47.

2. **Cut vertical triangles.**
   Cut triangles from vertical stripes following directions on page 47.

3. **Make solid triangles.**
   Measure the height of the horizontal fussy triangle.
   Cut the solid fabric strip the same height.
   Cut triangles as shown on page 12.

4. **Sew the quilt blocks.**
   Sew a horizontal fussy-cut triangle, right sides together, to a solid triangle.
   Press seam allowances toward the solid fabric.

5. **Square up the blocks, if necessary.**
   See page 88.

6. **Lay out the design.**
   There are several possibilities, including those shown on the following pages.
   The quilt blocks are also great for border strips.

Fussy-cuts
These do waste fabric, but with proper planning, the upside-down triangles can also be used in this project or in another one.

Yardages and sizes for Quilt Block 11 are on page 88.

Painted Desert

Finished size: 15-by-15 inches
A photo of the top left quilt, made
by Kaye Wood, is on page 46.

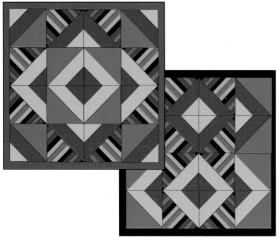

Fabric Requirements for Each Quilt

Horizontal combination strip:

Brown	Cut one 1 1/2-by-44-inch strip.
Light teal	Cut one 1 1/2-by-44-inch strip.
Stripe	Cut one 2 1/2-by-44-inch strip.
Solid	Cut one 2 1/2-by-44-inch strip.
Border	Cut two 2-by-44-inch strips.
Backing	17-by-17 inches
Batting	17-by-17 inches
Binding	Use two 1 3/4-by-44-inch strips.

Cut eight.

1 1/2 inches ➔
1 1/2 inches ➔ A   B

Cut eight.

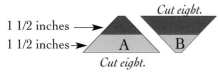

Cut eight.

Cut eight.

Sew four of each of these quilt blocks.

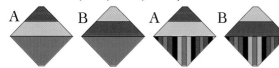

A   B   A   B

Quilt on left

Rows 1 and 4

Rows 2 and 3

Quilt on right

Rows 1 and 2

Rows 3 and 4

1. Make horizontal triangles.

Sew the two strips 1 1/2 inches wide.
Sew right sides together, into a combination strip.
Press seam allowances toward the darker fabric.
Cut eight "A" and eight "B" topless triangles with the Starmaker 8, following the instructions on page 28.

2. Cut vertical triangles.

Cut a stripe 2 1/2 inches high. See page 47.
Fussy-cut or random-cut into eight topless triangles.
See page 28.

3. Cut solid triangles.

Cut a strip 2 1/2 inches wide.
Cut eight topless triangles. See page 28.

4. Sew into quilt blocks.

Sew the triangles into quilt blocks (shown at left).

5. Sew into rows.

Match seamline where necessary. See page 12.
Press the seam allowances for each row in opposite directions.

6. Sew the rows together.

Match seamlines where necessary.
Press seam allowances open to reduce the bulk from so many seams coming together.

7. Finish.

Add mitered or square borders; see pages 90 and 91.
Cut two 2-by-44-inch strips.
Pin-mark to match seamlines. See page 89.
Press seam allowances toward the border strip.
Layer, quilt, add sleeve, and bind. See page 92.

Kokopelli Plays Again

Finished size: 76-by-102 inches
A photo of this quilt, made by Kaye Wood, is on page 53 and is also featured on the front cover.

Fabric Requirements for Each Quilt

Motif fabric	Enough for twenty 8 1/2-inch fussy-cut triangles. Minimum of 1 1/4 yards	
Triangles:		
Brown	1 yard	Cut four 8 1/2-by-44-inch strips.
Tan	1 yard	Cut three 8 1/2-by-44-inch strips.
Teal	1 yard	Cut four 8 1/2-by-44-inch strips.
Vertical strips	Enough for twenty-four fussy-cut triangles. Minimum of 2 1/2 yards	
First borders:		
Brown	1/2 yard	Cut six 2-by-44-inch strips.
Tan	1/4 yard	Cut four 2-by-44-inch strips.
Second border:		
	1 1/2 yards	Cut ten 4 1/2-by-44-inch strips.
Backing	80-by-110 inches	
Batting	80-by-110 inches	
Binding	2/3 yard	Cut ten 1 3/4-inch strips.

1. **Cut motif triangles**
   Cut twenty triangles, with the motif centered, the same height as the Starmaker 8 (8 1/2 inches). See page 43.

2. **Cut vertical triangles.**
   Cut the striped fabric into 8 1/2-inch-high strips. Fussy-cut twenty-four triangles by centering the point of the 4-angle of the Starmaker 8 on a particular stripe or strip. See page 48.

3. **Cut solid-colored triangles.**
   Cut three 8 1/2-by-44-inch tan strips.
   Cut four 8 1/2-by-44-inch brown strips.
   Cut four 8 1/2-by-44-inch teal strips.
   Cut into triangles as shown on page 11.

4. **Sew the following quilt blocks:**
   Sixteen motif triangles "A" to solid triangles "E" (Quilt Block 9).
   Four motif triangles "A" to solid triangles "C" (Quilt Block 9).
   Eight striped triangles "B" to solid triangles "C" (Quilt Block 11).
   Sixteen striped triangles "B" to solid triangles "D" (Quilt Block 11).

   Press the seam allowances toward the solid fabric.

A   Cut twenty.

B   Cut twenty-four.

C   Cut twelve.

D   Cut sixteen.

E   Cut sixteen.

Sew sixteen.

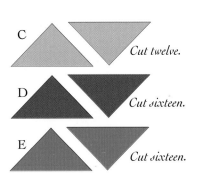

A   E

Sew four.   A   C

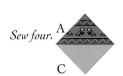

Sew eight.   *Sew sixteen.*

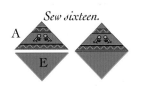

C   B   D

This Kokopelli fabric was perfect for my southwest quilt. Kokopelli is a legendary traveling salesman usually depicted playing a flute, possibly to alert a village that he was coming.

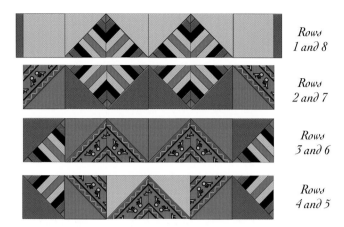

Cut four.

Rows 1 and 8

Rows 2 and 7

Rows 3 and 6

Rows 4 and 5

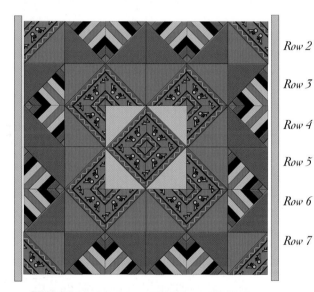

Row 2

Row 3

Row 4

Row 5

Row 6

Row 7

Completed Kokopelli quilt.

5. Cut squares.

Measure the finished quilt blocks. They should be approximately 11 1/2-by-11 1/2 inches.

Cut four squares this size.

6. Sew into rows.

Sew the rows together following the diagram at right.

The first border has an interesting division. Rows 1 and 8 have brown borders; sew a short brown sashing strip 2-by-11 1/2 inches to both ends. See page 89. Press the seam allowances of each row in opposite directions.

7. Sew rows 2 through 7.

Sew rows 2 through 7 together. Press seam allowances.

Rows 2 through 7 have tan side borders. Measure the length of rows 2 through 7. Cut four 2-inch tan border strips. Sew two strips together for each border to get the needed length. Pin-mark to match seamlines, following directions for long sashing strips on page 89.

Sew these strips to rows 2 through 7.

8. Sew all of the rows together.

9. Add the rest of the border strips.

The top and bottom brown border strips are cut 2 inches wide; sew two or more together to make the strip long enough. Pin-mark to match seamlines, in the same way the side borders are pinned. See page 89.

Cut the second border strips 4 1/2 inches wide; sew two or more together to make the strip long enough. Pin-mark. See page 89.

10. Finish.

Layer, quilt, and add binding. See page 92.

Chapter 6

Vertical Divided Triangles

Illusions, made by Kaye Wood. Directions on page 57.

Jewel, made by Kaye Wood. Directions on page 56.

Shadows, made by Brenda Jonsson. Directions on page 60.

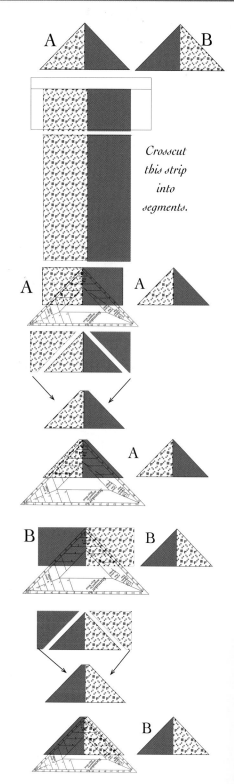

Crosscut this strip into segments.

1. Make combination strips.

Sew two equal width strips, right sides together, into a combination strip.

Press seam allowances toward the darker fabric.

2. Crosscut combination strip.

Crosscut this combination strip into equal segments, using the chart below for the measurements.

For example, if the combination strip is 9 1/2 inches wide, crosscut the combination strip into 4-inch segments.

3. Cut "A" triangles.

Cut these segments into "A" triangles by placing the point of the 4-angle of the Starmaker 8 at the top of the piece, centered on the seamline between the two fabrics. Line up the outside point and the inside point (see page 9) on the Starmaker 8 with the seamline.

A second "A" triangle can be cut from each crosscut.

Bring the two ends of each piece together, as shown.

Turn the end pieces and sew them together.

Cut an "A" triangle.

4. Cut "B" triangles.

Follow step 1 and 2 above.

Turn the segments upside-down before cutting the "B" triangles.

Continue with Step 3 above.

Vertical Divided Triangles

each strip	combination strip*	triangles crosscut	per strip
3 inches wide	5 1/2 inches	2 inches	42
4 inches wide	7 1/2 inches	3 inches	28
5 inches wide	9 1/2 inches	4 inches	20
6 inches wide	11 1/2 inches	5 inches	16
7 inches wide	13 1/2 inches	6 inches	14

*If your combination strip is *slightly* wider or narrower than the measurement listed above (because of a difference in seam allowances), it's okay. This technique will still work; yardages will be the same.

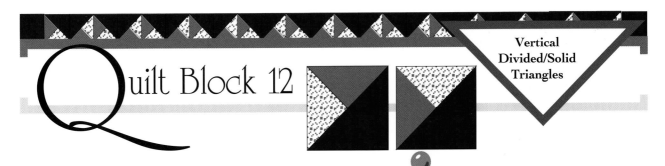

Quilt Block 12

1. **Vertical divided triangles.**
   Follow directions on page 54.

2. **Solid-colored triangles.**
   Cut solid strips the same width as the crosscut segments from page 54.
   Cut the solid strips into triangles, by placing the point of the 4-angle of the Starmaker 8 at the top of the strip; Cut the next triangle by turning the Starmaker upside-down with the point of the 4-angle at the bottom of the strip.

3. **Sew quilt blocks.**
   Sew a divided triangle "A" and or "B" to each solid triangle, depending on the design. Press seam allowances toward the solid-colored triangle.

4. **Square up the quilt blocks, if necessary.**
   See page 88.

5. **Lay out the design.**
   There are several possibilities, including those shown on the following pages.
   The designs are also great for border strips.

Embellishments
Show off your quilting or embroidery designs. The solid triangles are great for embellishing.

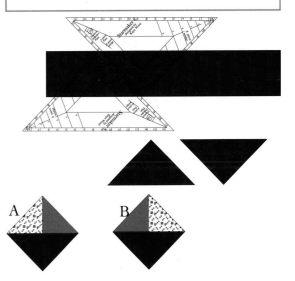

A   B

Vertical designs
These triangles can be combined with each other, or combined with solid or horizontal triangles.

Sizes for Quilt Blocks 12 and 13
Sizes for any vertical divided/triangle blocks

each strip	vertical combination strip	crosscut	block size	finished block size
3 inches wide	5 1/2 inches	2 inches	3 1/2 inches	3 inches
4 inches wide	7 1/2 inches	3 inches	4 inches	3 1/2 inches
5 inches wide	9 1/2 inches	4 inches	5 1/4 inches	4 3/4 inches
6 inches wide	11 1/2 inches	5 inches	6 3/4 inches	6 1/4 inches
7 inches wide	13 1/2 inches	6 inches	8 inches	7 1/2 inches

Jewel

Finished size: 61-by-80 inches
A photo of this quilt, made
by Kaye Wood, is on page 53.

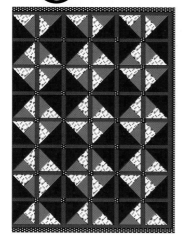

Cut forty-eight.

A

Cut forty-eight.

Sew forty-eight.

Fabric Requirements

Combination strips:

Light mauve	1 yard	Cut four 7-by-44-inch strips.
Mauve	1 yard	Cut four 7-by-44-inch strips.
Blue	1 1/2 yards	Cut eight 6-by-44-inch strips.
Sashing/first border	1 yard	Cut seventeen 2-by-44-inch strips.
Sashing squares		Cut two 2-by-44-inch strips.
Second border	1 yard	Cut eight 3 1/4-inch strips.
Backing	65-by-85 inches	
Batting	65-by-85 inches	
Binding	1/2 yard	Cut 1 3/4-inch strips.

1. Make divided triangles.

Sew the two 7-inch strips, right sides together, into four combination strips. Crosscut these strips into twenty-four 6-inch segments and cut forty-eight "A" triangles. Directions are on page 54.

2. Cut solid triangles.

Cut blue strips into forty-eight triangles. Directions for Quilt Block 12 are on page 55.

3. Sew quilt blocks.

Sew a dark triangle to each "A" vertical divided triangle.

4. Make short sashing strips.

Cut the 2-inch sashing strips into forty 2-by-8-inch pieces.
Sew six blocks and sashing strips into rows.
Follow directions for short sashing strips on page 89.

5. Make long sashing strips.

Cut the 2-inch sashing strips into forty-two 2-by-8-inch pieces.
Sashing squares: Cut the 2-inch strips into thirty-five 2-inch squares.
Sew seven long sashing strips, each with six 8-inch strips and five 2-inch squares.

6. Sew rows together.

Sew together by alternating a row of quilt blocks with a long sashing strip. Match seamlines.

7. Finish.

Borders: Sew two sashing or border strips together to make the strip long enough. Match seamlines. Press seam allowances toward the border strip. Layer, quilt, and bind. See page 92.

Illusions

Finished size: 30-by-30 inches
A photo of this quilt, made
by Kaye Wood, is on page 53.

Fabric Requirements

Combination strip:

Light mauve	1/2 yard	Cut two 7-by-44-inch strips.
Mauve	1/2 yard	Cut two 7-by-44-inch strips.
Blue	1/2 yard	Cut three 6-by-44-inch strips.
Backing	1 yard	
Batting	36-by-36 inches	

Embellishments!
Try adding a decorative trim or lace doily in the solid triangles.

1. Make divided triangles.
   Sew 7-inch strips, right sides together, into
   two combination strips.
   Crosscut this strip into 6-inch segments. Cut
   ten "A" triangles and six "B" triangles.
   Directions are on page 54.

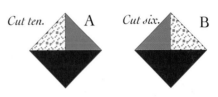

Cut ten. **A**   Cut six. **B**

2. Cut solid triangles.
   Cut sixteen triangles from the blue strips,
   following directions on page 55.

3. Sew quilt blocks.
   Sew a dark triangle to each "A" and "B" verti-
   cal divided triangle.
   Directions for Quilt Block 12 are on page 55.

Rows 1 and 4

Rows 2 and 3

4. Sew into rows.
   Sew four rows, as shown at right.

5. Sew rows together.
   Match seamlines. See
   page 12.

6. Finish.
   Layer, quilt, and bind.
   See page 92.

Same design, different fabrics!

Different design, same blocks!

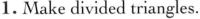
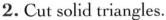

Try these designs, all made from "A" and "B" divided triangle blocks.

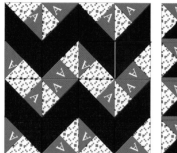
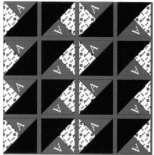

Both of these wallhangings are made from sixteen "A" divided triangle blocks.

The blocks in the quilt on the near left are divided by sashing strips.

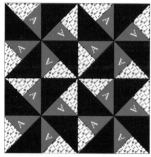
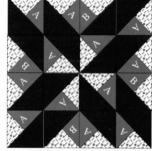

These wallhangings are made from sixteen "A" and "B" divided triangle blocks.

More embellishments!

Show off your quilting in the large triangles.

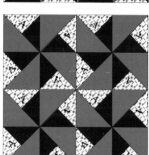

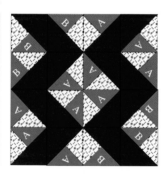

On-point quilt blocks look entirely different.

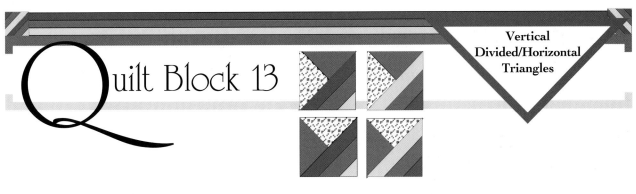

Quilt Block 13

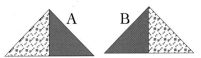

1. Cut vertical divided triangles.

Cut "A" and "B" triangles. See directions on page 54.

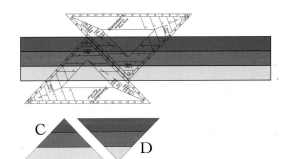

2. Make horizontal stripped triangles.

Sew strips together into a combination strip that equals the height of the segments from which the "A" and "B" triangles were cut. See page 54.

Cut into triangles, by placing the point of the 4-angle of the Starmaker 8 at the top of the strip. Cut the next triangle by turning the Starmaker upside-down with the point of the 4-angle at the bottom of the strip.

Mix and match.
Five different fabrics can be used in each of these quilts.

3. Sew quilt blocks.

Sew a divided triangle "A" or "B" to a horizontal triangle "C" or "D," depending on the design.
Press seam allowances toward the horizontal triangle.

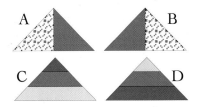

4. Square up the quilt blocks, if necessary.

See page 88.

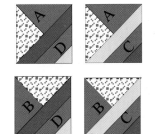

5. Lay out the design.

There are several possibilities, including those shown on the following pages.
The quilt blocks are also great for border strips.

Yardages and sizes for Quilt Block 13 are on page 55.

Shadows

Finished size: 36-by-36 inches
A photo of this quilt, made
by Brenda Jonsson, is on page 53.

Cut eight.

Cut eight.

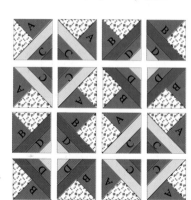

Fabric Requirements

Divided triangles:
    Light mauve Cut one 6-by-44-inch strip.
    Mauve   Cut one 6-by-44-inch strip.
Horizontal stripped triangles:
    Pink   Cut two 2-by-44-inch strips.
    Mauve   Cut two 2-by-44-inch strips.
  Purple   Cut two 2-by-44-inch strips.
  Backing   1 1/4 yard
  Batting   40-by-40 inches
    (optional for table covers)

Tablecovers
These make perfect gifts!

1. Make divided triangles.

Sew the 6-inch strips from the light and medium fabrics, right sides together, to make one 11 1/2-inch-wide combination strip.

Crosscut this strip into 5-inch segments. Cut eight "A" triangles and eight "B" triangles.

Directions are on page 54.

2. Make horizontal triangles.

Sew a light, medium, and dark fabric together to make two 5-inch combination strips.

Press seam allowances toward the darkest fabric. Cut eight "C" and eight "D" triangles. See page 59.

3. Sew quilt blocks.

Sew eight "AC" blocks and eight "BD" blocks. Directions for Quilt Block 13 are on page 59.

4. Sew into rows.

Lay out the blocks in this design, or try one of your own designs.

Sew four quilt blocks in each row.

Match seamlines. See page 12.

5. Sew rows together

Sew into four rows, as shown at right.

Match seamlines.

6. Finish.

Layer, quilt, and bind.

See page 92.

Chapter 7
Vertical and Horizontal
Triangles

Hawaiian Fantasy (top left) and Spring Rain (lower left), made by Brenda Jonsson. Directions on pages 64 and 67, respectively.
Floral Windows (top right) and Crossroads (lower right), made by Kaye Wood. Directions on pages 65 and 71, respectively.

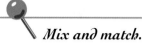

Vertical and horizontal triangles can be cut from the same combination strip. An overall design, such as a large floral, is best for the wide center stripe.

1. Make combination strips.

Sew an odd number of strips (three, five, seven, etc.) into a combination strip.

The two outside strips are the same width; these strips and the center motif strip should be at least 3 inches wide. The strips on both sides of the center should be the same fabric and the same width. Inside strips can be narrower (from 1 to 2 inches). Press seam allowances away from the center motif strip.

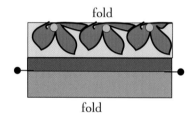

2. Cut squares.

Cut the combination strip into squares.

For example, if the combination strip is 10 inches wide, cut it into 10-by-10-inch squares. If it is 13 1/2 inches wide, cut it into 13 1/2-by-13 1/2-inch squares.

fold

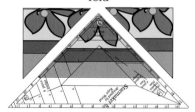

fold

3. Fold the strip.

Fold the strip along the center of the motif strip. Press the center fold.

Pin seamlines together at the ends of the combination strip to keep the two layers from shifting.

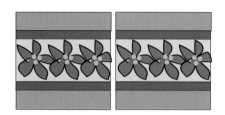

4. Cut triangles.

Place the Starmaker 8 with the point of the 4-angle at the fold.

Cut along both edges of the Starmaker.

From one square, four triangles will be cut: two vertical and two horizontal.

Two horizontal triangles. *From each square:* *Two vertical triangles.*

Sizes for Vertical/Horizontal Triangles		
combination strip	square	height of triangles
8 inches	8 inches	4 inches
9 inches	9 inches	4 1/2 inches
10 inches	10 inches	5 inches
11 inches	11 inches	5 1/2 inches
12 inches	12 inches	6 inches
13 inches	13 inches	6 1/2 inches
14 inches	14 inches	7 inches
15 inches	15 inches	7 1/2 inches
16 inches	16 inches	8 inches
17 inches	17 inches	8 1/2 inches

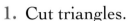

Quilt Blocks 14 and 15

Quilt Block 14   *Quilt Block 15*
Vertical triangles.   *Horizontal triangles.*

1. Cut triangles.

Cut both vertical and horizontal triangles at the same time—and make both Quilt Blocks 14 and 15.

See page 62.

2. Sew quilt blocks.

Sew four vertical triangles together to make Quilt Block 14.

Sew four horizontal triangles together to make Quilt Block 15.

First sew two triangles together, matching seamlines, to make half of each quilt block. Press seam allowances on each half in opposite directions.

Sew two halves together, matching seamlines, to make the quilt block.

Vertical triangles.   *Horizontal triangles.*

3. Square up these blocks.

Especially if the two different blocks are to be used in the same project, they must be the same size.

See page 62.

4. Lay out the design.

There are several possibilities, including those shown on the following pages.

Yardages and sizes for Quilt Blocks 14 and 15 are on page 62.

Hawaiian Fantasy

Finished size: 34-by-34 inches
A photo of this quilt, made by
Brenda Jonsson, is on page 61.

Fabric Requirements

Floral motif stripe	1 yard	
Borders	1/4 yard	Cut four 2-by-44-inch strips.
Backing	36-by-36 inches	
Batting	36-by-36 inches	
Binding	1/4 yard	Cut four 3-by-44-inch strips.

Did you know?

It is against the law to leave a state without buying fabric.
The stripes on this Hawaiian fabric were perfect for this design.
Only the one stripe was used for the quilt blocks.

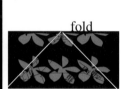

1. **Cut stripes.**
   Cut two stripes 17 inches wide.
   Cut the stripes into four 17-inch squares. See page 62.

fold

2. **Cut triangles.**
   Fold the strip and cut eight vertical triangles and eight horizontal side triangles. See page 62.

Eight vertical triangles.   *Eight horizontal triangles.*

Sew two.
vertical blocks.

Sew two.
horizontal blocks.

3. **Sew quilt blocks.**
   Sew four vertical triangles together to make each Quilt Block 14.
   Sew four horizontal triangles together to make each Quilt Block 15. See page 63.

4. **Sew into rows.**
   Sew one Quilt Block 14 and one Quilt Block 15 together for each row.
   Press seam allowances in opposite directions.

5. **Sew rows together.**
   Match seamlines, and press seam allowances.

6. **Finish.**
   Add mitered or square borders; see pages 90 and 91. Pin-mark the border strips to match seamlines and control the bias edges. See page 89. Press seam allowances toward the border strip. Layer, quilt, and add sleeve; see page 92. Cut binding strips 3-by-44 inches for a 1/2-inch finished binding. See page 92.

Floral Windows

Finished size: 40-by-40 inches
A photo of this quilt, made by
Kaye Wood, is on page 61.

Fabric Requirements

Combination strip:

Floral motif	2/3 yard	Cut four 5 1/2-by-44-inch strips.
Dark	1/2 yard	Cut eight 2-by-44-inch strips.
Medium	2/3 yard	Cut eight 3-by-44-inch strips.
Borders	1/4 yard	Cut four 2-by-44-inch strips.
Backing/sleeve	1 1/2 yards	
Batting	43-by-43 inches	
Binding	1/4 yard	Cut into 1 3/4-inch strips.

1. Make combination strips.

Cut a strip 13 1/2 inches wide, or sew combination strips together as follows: 3 inches to 2 inches to 5 1/2 inches to 2 inches to 3 inches.

Press seam allowances away from the center (5 1/2-inch) strip.

Measure the width of the combination strip. It should be approximately 13 1/2 inches; however, use your measurement to cut the combination strips into ten squares. See page 62.

2. Cut triangles.

Cut twenty vertical triangles and twenty horizontal side triangles.

Only sixteen of the vertical triangles will be used in the quilt. Use the four remaining vertical triangles to make a coordinating pillow.

Cut twenty.

Cut twenty.

3. Sew quilt blocks.

Sew four vertical triangles together to make each Quilt Block 14.

Sew four horizontal triangles together to make each Quilt Block 15. See page 63.

Sew four. *Sew five.*

4. Sew into rows.

Sew three quilt blocks together into three rows. Press seam allowances in opposite directions.

5. Sew rows together.

Match seamlines, and press seam allowances.

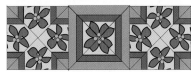

6. Finish.

Add mitered or square borders; pages 90 and 91.

Pin-mark the border strips to match seamlines. See page 89.

Press seam allowances toward the border strip.

Layer, quilt, and add sleeve and binding. See page 92.

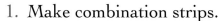

1. **Make combination strips.**
   Sew an odd number of strips (three, five, seven, etc.) into a combination strip.
   Press seam allowances away from the center motif fabric.
   See page 62 for more information.
   Or use a geometric stripe instead of sewing a combination strip.

Vertical triangles.   *Horizontal triangles.*

2. **Cut triangles.**
   Cut vertical and horizontal triangles, as shown on page 62.
   Both triangles are cut at the same time.

3. **Sew the quilt blocks.**
   Sew a vertical triangle to a horizontal triangle to make each quilt block.
   Press seam allowances toward the horizontal triangle.

4. **Square up blocks, if necessary.**
   See page 88.

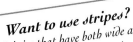

Want to use stripes?
Look for fabrics that have both wide and narrow vertical stripes. The motif fabric should be wide enough to make a real statement in your quilt.

Yardages and sizes for Quilt Block 16 are on page 62.

Spring Rain

Finished size: 22 1/2-by-22 1/2 inches
A photo of this quilt, made by
Brenda Jonsson, is on page 61.

Fabric Requirements for Each Quilt

Combination strips:

Floral	1/2 yard	Cut three 5-by-44-inch strips.
Dark	1/4 yard	Cut six 1 1/2-by-44-inch strips.
Medium	1/2 yard	Cut six 3-by-44-inch strips.
First border	1/3 yard	Cut four 2 1/2-by-44-inch strips.
Second border		
	1/4 yard	Cut four 1 1/2-by-44-inch strips.
Backing	40-by-40 inches	
Batting	40-by-40 inches	
Binding	1/4 yard	Cut 1 3/8-inch strips.

1. **Make combination strips.**
   Cut a stripe or sew combination strips
   together as follows: 3 inches to 1 1/2 inches to
   5 inches to 1 1/2 inches to 3 inches.
   Cut the combination strip into squares. See
   page 62.

2. **Cut triangles.**
   Cut sixteen vertical and sixteen horizontal tri-
   angles.
   See page 62.

Cut sixteen.

*Vertical
triangles.*

*Horizontal
triangles.*

3. **Sew quilt blocks.**
   Sew sixteen vertical/horizontal triangle quilt
   blocks.
   Follow directions on page 66 for Quilt Block
   16.

Sew sixteen.

4. **Sew into rows.**
   Sew four quilt blocks together into four identi-
   cal rows.
   Turn every other row upside-down.
   Press seam allowances in opposite directions.

Quilt on bottom.

5. **Sew rows together.**
   Match seamlines, and press seam allowances.

6. **Finish.**
   Add mitered or square borders. See pages 90
   and 91.
   Press seam allowances toward the border
   strip.
   Layer, quilt, and add sleeve and binding. See
   page 92.

Quilt on top.

Quilt Blocks 17 and 18

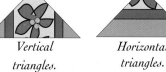

Quilt Block 17
*Vertical/Solid
Triangles.*

Quilt Block 18
*Horizontal/Solid
Triangles.*

*Vertical
triangles.*

*Horizontal
triangles.*

1. Cut triangles.

Cut vertical and horizontal triangles, as shown on page 62. Both triangles are cut at the same time.

2. Cut solid triangles.

Measure the height of the triangles.

Cut the solid fabric the same width.

Cut this strip into triangles, by placing the point of the 4-angle of the Starmaker 8 at the top of the strip. Cut the next triangle by turning the Starmaker upside-down with the point of the 4-angle at the bottom of the strip

3. Sew the quilt blocks.

Sew a vertical or horizontal triangle to each solid triangle.

Press seam allowances toward the solid triangle.

4. Square up blocks, if necessary.

See page 88.

Embellishments
Add a decorative lace motif in the solid triangles.

*Yardages and sizes for Quilt Blocks 17 and 18
are on page 62.*

Dream Catchers

Finished size: 24-by-24 inches

Fabric Requirements for Both Quilts Combined

Combination strip:

Floral motif	Cut one 5-by-26-inch strip.
Dark	Cut two 1 1/2-by-26-inch strips.
Medium	Cut two 3-by-26-inch strips
Solid triangles	1/4 yard
Border	Cut four 1 1/2-by-26-inch strips.
Backing	8-by-28 inches
Batting	28-by-28 inches
Binding	Four 1 3/4-inch strips

1. **Make combination strips.**

   Cut a stripe, or sew combination strips together as follows: 3 inches to 1 1/2 inches to 5 inches to 1 1/2 inches to 3 inches. Press seam allowances away from the center (5-inch) strip.

   Measure the width of the combination strip. It should be approximately 12 inches. Use your measurement to cut the combination strips into two squares. See page 62.

2. **Cut triangles.**

   Cut four vertical and four horizontal triangles. See page 62.

   Cut eight solid triangles. See page 68, Quilt Blocks 17 and 18.

Cut 4.   *Cut 4.*

Horizontal triangles.   *Vertical triangles.*

3. **Sew quilt blocks.**

   Sew four vertical triangles to four solid triangles.
   Sew four horizontal triangles to four solid triangles
   Follow directions on page 68, Quilt Blocks 17 and 18.

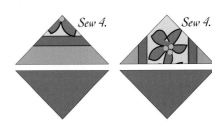

Sew 4.   *Sew 4.*

4. **Sew into rows.**

   Sew two quilt blocks together into two identical rows.
   Turn the second row upside-down.
   Press seam allowances in opposite directions.

5. **Sew rows together.**

   Match seamlines, and press seam allowances.

Quilt on top.   *Quilt on bottom.*

6. **Finish.**

   Add mitered or square borders; pages 90 and 91.
   Pin-mark the border strips to match seamlines. See page 89.
   Press seam allowances toward the border strip.
   Layer, quilt, and add sleeve and binding. See page 92.

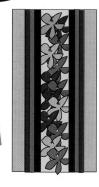

Diamonds

Cut diamonds whenever your motif fabric would look better in one piece instead of sewing two horizontal triangles together with a seam down the middle.

1. **Sew combination strips.**

   Sew an odd number of strips (three, five, seven, etc.) into a combination strip.

   The two outside strips and the center motif strip should be at least 3 inches wide.

   Inside strips should be narrower (from 1 to 2 inches).

   Press seam allowances away from the center motif strip.

2. **Fold combination strips.**

   Fold the strip along the center of the motif strip. Press the center fold.

   Pin seamlines together at the ends and in the middle of the combination strip to keep the two layers from shifting.

3. **Cut triangles.**

   Place the Starmaker 8 with the point of the 4-angle at the raw edges (the side opposite the fold).

   Cut along both edges of the Starmaker.

   From one square, a diamond and two horizontal triangles will be cut.

   The horizontal triangles can be used in any of the designs in this book that call for horizontal triangles, such as:

Step 2   *Step 3* Fold

Fold

Quilt Block 1, see page 13.

Quilt Block 2, see page 16.

Quilt Block 5, see page 27.

Sizes for Diamonds

combination strip	width of diamonds	height of triangles
8 inches	8 inches	4 inches
9 inches	9 inches	4 1/2 inches
10 inches	10 inches	5 inches
11 inches	11 inches	5 1/2 inches
12 inches	12 inches	6 inches
13 inches	13 inches	6 1/2 inches
14 inches	14 inches	7 inches
15 inches	15 inches	7 1/2 inches
16 inches	16 inches	8 inches
17 inches	17 inches	8 1/2 inches

Crossroads

Finished size: 34-by-34 inches
A photo of this quilt, made by
Kaye Wood, is on page 61.

Fabric Requirements

Combination strip:

Floral	1/2 yard	Cut two 6 1/2-by-44 inch strips.
Dark	1/8 yard	Cut two 1 1/2-by-44-inch strips.
Medium	1/8 yard	Cut two 1 1/2-by-44-inch strips.
Medium	1/8 yard	Cut two 1 1/2-by-44-inch strips.
Light	1/8 yard	Cut two 2-by-44-inch strips.
Corner triangles	1/2 yard	
Border	1/2 yard	Cut four 3-by-44-inch strips.
Backing	1 yard	
Batting	36-by-36 inches	
Binding	1/4 yard	Cut 1 3/4-inch strips.

1. **Make combination strips.**

   Sew two combination strips, right sides together, each
   with the following strips: 2 inches to 1 1/2 inches to
   1 1/2 inches to 1 1/2 inches to 6 1/2 inches to 1 1/2
   inches to 1 1/2 inches to 1 1/2 inches to 2 inches.

2. **Cut diamonds.**

   Cut four diamonds. See page 70 for cutting Quilt
   Block 19.
   Use the horizontal triangles for coordinating pillows.

3. **Sew into rows.**

   Sew two quilt blocks together into two rows, matching seamlines.
   Press seam allowances in opposite directions.

4. **Sew rows together.**

   Match seamlines.

5. **Finish.**

   Corner triangles. Cut two 16-inch squares from the
   triangle fabric. Cut diagonally through both squares
   to get the four triangles needed for the corners.
   Pin-mark the center and edges along the diagonal
   side of these triangles, following the directions for
   pin-marking sashing strips. See page 89.
   Sew the diagonal side of each triangle to each side of
   the quilt, matching seamlines to pins.
   Square up the quilt 1/4 inches beyond the points of
   the diamond.
   Press seam allowances toward the triangles.
   Add a mitered border. See page 91.
   Layer, quilt, and add sleeve and binding. See page 92.

Looks like a cross ...
This would be perfect for a liturgical banner for the Easter holiday season.

Cut four.

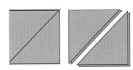

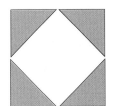

Chapter 8

Up-and-Down Triangles

Both quilts—Chill Out (above) and Mike's Quilt (right)—were made by Brenda Jonsson. Directions are on pages 75 and 76, respectively.

Fabric used for the up-and-down triangles can be an overall print, such as a one-directional floral vine or the wolf fabric in Mike's Quilt, or a fussy-cut motif. The design will be vertical (up and down) in the triangle.

1. Cut strip the desired width (up to 12 inches high).

2. Cut triangles.
   "C" triangle: Place the bottom of the Starmaker 8 along the bottom of the strip. The diagonal side of the Starmaker 8 should go to the corner, regardless of the width of the strip, see diagram below on left.
   "D" triangle: Turn the Starmaker 8 so the bottom of the Starmaker is now at the top of the strip. The vertical side of the Starmaker should go to the lower corner, regardless of the width of the strip.
   "E" triangle: The bottom of the Starmaker 8 is now at the top of the strip.
   The diagonal side of the Starmaker 8 should go to the lower corner.
   "F" triangle: Turn the Starmaker 8 so the bottom is now at the bottom of the strip.
   The vertical side of the Starmaker should go to the upper corner.

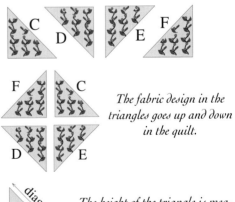

The design goes up and down.
The design will be up and down inside the triangle. Strips can be any height.

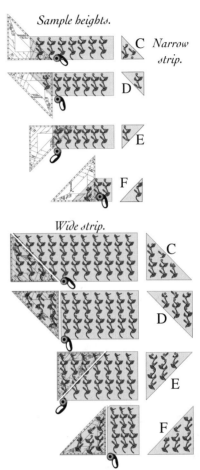

Sample heights.

C Narrow strip.

D

E

F

Wide strip.

C

D

E

F

If you cut two "C" and "D" triangles but only one "E" and one "F" triangle from a strip, start the second strip by cutting "E" and "F" triangle.

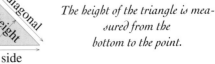

The fabric design in the triangles goes up and down in the quilt.

The height of the triangle is measured from the bottom to the point.

Sizes for Up-and-Down Triangles

strip width	*height	diagonal	side
5 inches	5 inches	3 1/2 inches	7 inches
6 inches	6 inches	4 1/4 inches	8 1/2 inches
7 inches	7 inches	5 inches	10 inches
8 inches	8 inches	5 5/8 inches	11 3/8 inches
9 inches	9 inches	6 1/2 inches	13 inches
10 inches	10 inches	7 inches	14 inches
11 inches	11 inches	7 3/4 inches	15 1/2 inches
12 inches	12 inches	8 1/2 inches	17 inches

*The height of the triangle is the measurement needed to combine

Quilt Block 20

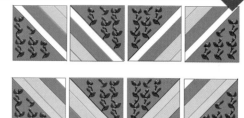
Lots of choices.

Four triangles are cut from one vertical strip — combine these with two different horizontal triangles, and you get eight different quilt blocks.

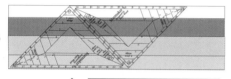

C   D   E   F

side   height   diagonal

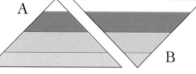

A

B

1. Cut up-and-down triangles.
   Cutting directions are on page 73.

2. Make horizontal triangles.
   Sew strips together into a combination strip that equals the height of the vertical triangle. See page 73.

   Cut the combination strip into triangles by placing the point of the 4-angle of the Starmaker 8 at the top of the strip. Cut the next triangle by turning the Starmaker upside-down with the point of the 4-angle at the bottom of the strip.

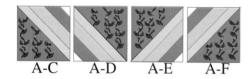

A-C   A-D   A-E   A-F

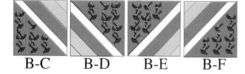

B-C   B-D   B-E   B-F

3. Sew eight different quilt blocks.
   Sew an "A" triangle to each of the up-and-down triangles "C," "D," "E," and "F."

   Sew a "B" triangle to each of the up-and-down triangles "C," "D," "E," and "F."

side   height   diagonal

Up-and-Down/Horizontal Triangles Size Chart

See page 73.

To use the chart on page 73, use the height of the triangle for the strip width.

Chill Out

It's an air conditioner cover!

Finished size: 31-by-31 inches
A photo of the finished quilt, made by
Brenda Jonsson, is on page 72.

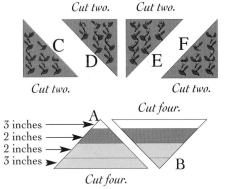

Fabric Requirements for Both Quilts

Up-and-down motif fabric 2/3 yard
Horizontal combination strips:

White		Cut two 3-by-44-inch strips.
Green		Cut two 2-by-44-inch strips.
Pink		Cut two 2-by-44-inch strips.
Light green		Cut two 3-by-44-inch strips.
Sashing		Cut two 1 1/2-by-44-inch strips.
First border	1/2 yard	Cut eight 2-by-44-inch strips.
Second border	1/2 yard	Cut eight 3-by-44-inch strips.
Backing		Cut two 34-by-34-inch pieces.
Batting		Cut two 34-by-34-inch pieces.
Binding	1/2 yard	Cut 1 3/4-inch strips.

1. Cut up-and-down triangles.
Cut two strips 12 inches wide from the motif fabric. Cut two of each triangle — "C," "D," "E," and "F." See page 73.

Cut two.   Cut two.

C
D   F
E

Cut two.   Cut two.

2. Make horizontal triangles.
Sew two combination strips, as shown: 3 inches to 2 inches to 2 inches to 3 inches.
Cut four "A" and four "B" triangles from the combination strips using the Starmaker 8. See Quilt Block 20, page 74.

Cut four.

3 inches →
2 inches →
2 inches →
3 inches →

A
B

Cut four.

3. Sew quilt blocks.
For the quilt on the left, sew "A" triangles to each of the four vertical triangles. For a variation, sew "B" triangles to each of the four vertical triangles.

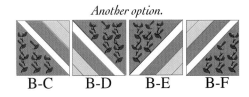

Quilt at top of page.

A-C   A-D   A-E   A-F

Another option.

B-C   B-D   B-E   B-F

4. Make short sashing strips.
For each quilt, cut two sashing strips 1 1/2-by-11 1/2 inches (or size of quilt block). Sew a sashing strip between two blocks. See page 89.
Press seam allowances toward the sashing strips.

5. Make long sashing strips.
For each quilt, cut two sashing strips 1 1/2-by-24 inches. To match seamlines, pin-mark the sashing strip. See page 89.
Sew the sashing strip, matching seamlines to pins.
Press seam allowances toward the sashing strips.

6. Finish.
Add borders. See page 89. Cut border strips 2 inches wide. To miter borders, sew both borders together before sewing them to the quilt top. Pin-mark to match seamlines. See page 89. Press seam allowances toward the border strip. Layer and quilt. See page 92.

Mike's Quilt

Finished size: 52-by-102 inches
A photo of this quilt, made by
Brenda Jonsson (Mike's mom), is on page 72.

Fabric Requirements

Up-and-down motif 2 yards (more for fussy-cuts)
Horizontal combination strips:

Beige	2/3 yard	Cut eight 2 1/2-by-44-inch strips.
Brown	2/3 yard	Cut eight 2 1/2-by-44-inch strips.
Rust	2/3 yard	Cut eight 2 1/2-by-44-inch strips.
Green	2/3 yard	Cut eight 2 1/2-by-44-inch strips.
Sashing	1 1/2 yard	Cut twenty-four 2-by-44-inch strips.
Borders	2/3 yard	Cut ten 2-by-44-inch strips.
Backing	55-by-105 inches	
Batting	55-by-105 inches	

1. Cut up-and-down triangles.
> Cut six strips 12 inches wide from the motif fabric.
> Cut eight of each triangle—"C," "D," "E," and "F." See page 73.

Cut eight of each.

2. Horizontal stripped triangles.
> Sew eight combination strips, each made from four 2 1/2-inch strips.
> Press seam allowances all in one direction. It will be slightly wider than the Starmaker 8.

Cut sixteen of each.

> Cut sixteen "A" triangles with the bottom of the Starmaker along the bottom of the combination strip.
> Cut sixteen "B" triangles with the bottom of the Starmaker 8 along the top of the combination strip.

Sew four of each block.

3. Sew quilt blocks.
> Sew four each of the eight blocks shown. See Quilt Block 20, page 74.

4. Make sashing strips.
> Cut long sashing strips first; cut fourteen 2-by-44-inch strips.
> Sew two strips together to make seven longer strips; cut these longer strips into seven 2-by-52-inch strips, with the seam in the middle.
> Cut twenty-eight short sashing strips 2-by-11 1/2-inches (or the size of the block). Some of the short sashing strips can be cut from leftover long sashing strip pieces.

5. Sew into rows
> Sew blocks and short sashing strips together in rows. See page 89.

Rows 1, 4, 5, and 8

Rows 2, 3, 6, and 7

6. Sew rows together.
> Pin-mark the three long sashing strips. See page 89.
> Sew the rows and sashing strips together.

7. Finish.
> Add mitered or square borders. See pages 90 and 91.
> Sew two or three border strips together to make them long enough.
> Pin-mark the border strips the same way as Step 6 above. See page 89.
> Press seam allowances toward the border strip.
> Layer and quilt.

Chapter 9

Flying Geese Triangles

The Geese Are Flying Along the Borders (top), made by Kaye Wood.
The Geese Are Flying North, South, East, and West, made by Brenda Jonsson.
Directions on pages 80 and 81, respectively.

$\mathcal{Q}$uilt Block 21

Flying Geese

Use them as borders, or create a whole quilt from them.

No fabric waste and no math!

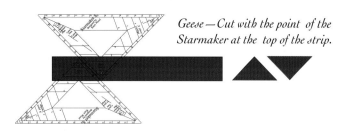

Geese—Cut with the point of the Starmaker at the top of the strip.

Background—Cut with the first line of the Starmaker at the top of the strip.

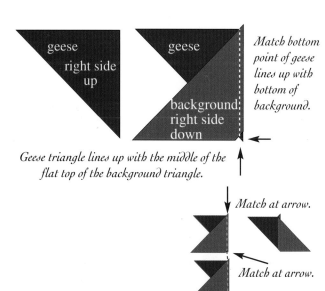

geese right side up

geese

background: right side down

Match bottom point of geese lines up with bottom of background.

Geese triangle lines up with the middle of the flat top of the background triangle.

Match at arrow.

Match at arrow.

Chain-stitch between triangles.

To easily strip-cut the geese:

1. **Cut strips.**
   Cut a dark and a light strip the same width. One strip will become the background (teal); the other the geese (brown).

2. **Cut the geese.**
   Cut the geese strip by placing the point of the 4-angle of the Starmaker 8 at the top of the strip and cutting. Cut the second triangle by turning the Starmaker 8 upside-down with the point of the 4-angle at the bottom of the strip.

3. **Cut the background.**
   Cut the background strip into triangles by placing the first line from the 4-angle at the top of the strip and cutting. Cut the second triangle by turning the Starmaker 8 upside-down with the 1st line from the 4-angle at the bottom of the strip.

4. **Sew triangles into strips.**
   Sew a geese triangle to a background triangle, the background triangle on top, and the geese underneath. Match the triangles where they overlap; see the arrows on the diagram. Chain-sew these two triangles together.
   Press seam allowances away from geese and toward background triangle.

Chain-sew together these triangle sets, with the same background fabric, to form groups of four triangles; then groups of eight triangles.

Geese segments can be cut from this strip (see step 5), and then more triangles can be added to both ends of the strip.

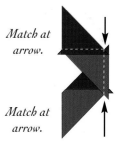

Match at arrow.

Match at arrow.

points

points

The strip will look like the one above:

> The seamlines on the points of the geese (brown) will match 1/4 inch from the top of the strip. The seamlines on the points of the background will meet at the edge of the strip. This will give the seam allowance needed to cut the background triangles to make Flying Geese.

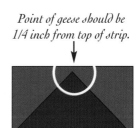

Point of geese should be 1/4 inch from top of strip.

Chain- stitch.

5. Cut Flying Geese.

Line up the Starmaker 8, as shown, with the side of the Starmaker 8 at the top of the strip, 4-angle at the center of the background triangle, and the #1, #2, and #3 lines on the Starmaker parallel to the seamline.

Cut one of the center Flying Geese by cutting the background triangle in half along the side of the Starmaker 8 (see dotted lines). Move the cut-off triangles from one end of the strip to the other end. Cut more Flying Geese blocks.

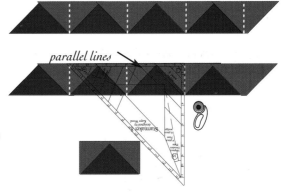

parallel lines

6. Continue to add and cut more geese and background triangles to the strip as needed.

Move the cut-off end to the other end of strip, and continue cutting geese.

Number of Triangles from Each Strip		
Strip width	Geese	Background
2 inches	19	16
3 inches	12	11
4 inches	9	9
5 inches	7	6
6 inches	6	5
7 inches	5	4
8 inches	4	4

Flying Geese Blocks		
Strip width	Width	Length
2 inches	1 7/8 inches	3 1/4 inches
3 inches	2 7/8 inches	5 1/4 inches
4 inches	3 7/8 inches	7 1/4 inches
5 inches	4 7/8 inches	9 1/4 inches
6 inches	5 7/8 inches	11 1/4 inches
7 inches	6 7/8 inches	13 1/4 inches

The Geese are Flying Along the Borders

Finished size: 39 1/2-by-28 1/2 inches
A photo of this quilt, by Kaye Wood, is on page 77.

Fabric Requirements

Geese	2/3 yard	Cut seven 3-by-44-inch strips.
Dark background	1//2 yard	Cut four 3-by-44-inch strips.
Light background	1/3 yard	Cut three 3-by-44-inch strips.
Sashing	1/3 yard	Cut six 1 1/2-by-44-inch strips.
Backing/sleeve	1 yard	
Batting	41-by-32 inches	
Binding	1/4 yard	

Cut eighty-four.

Cut forty-eight.

Cut thirty-six.

1. Cut triangles.

Cut eighty-four triangles from the 3-inch geese fabric strips.

Cut forty-eight background triangles from the 3-inch dark strips. Cut thirty-six background triangles from the 3-inch light strips. Directions are on page 78.

2. Sew Flying Geese strips.

Directions are on page 78.

Sew a strip of geese (brown) and dark background.

Sew a strip of geese (brown) and light background.

Forty-eight dark blocks.

Thirty-six light blocks.

3. Cut Flying Geese blocks.

Cut forty-eight blocks with dark background, and cut thirty-six blocks with light background.

Rows 1 and 7 Rows 2 and 6 Rows 3 and 5 Row 4

4. Sew into vertical rows.

Sew twelve Flying Geese blocks into each row, as shown.

The top points of the geese (brown) should come right to the seamline.

5. Make sashing strips.

Cut sashing strips.

Pin-mark to match the sashing strips at the center and both ends of the strips. See page 89.

Press seam allowances toward the sashing strip.

6. Finish.

Layer, quilt, add sleeve, and bind. See page 92.

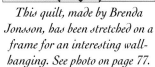

The Geese are Flying North, South, East and West

Finished size: 19-by-19 inches

Fabric Requirements for Each Quilt

Geese	Cut one 3-by-44-inch strip.
Background:	
Dark	Cut one 3-by-22-inch strip.
Medium	Cut one 3-by-22-inch strip.
Light	Cut one 3-by-22-inch strip.
Large corner triangles:	
Dark	Cut one 8-by-44-inch strip.
Light	Cut one 8-by-44-inch strip.
Center square	6-by-6 inches
Backing	22-by-22 inches
Stretcher frame (for mounting)	
Batting	22-by-22 inches
Binding	2 1/4 yards

This quilt, made by Brenda Jonsson, has been stretched on a frame for an interesting wall-hanging. See photo on page 77.

1. **Cut Flying Geese triangles.**
   For each quilt:
   Cut twelve triangles from the 3-inch geese strip.
   Cut four triangles from each of the three background fabrics. See page 78.

Cut twelve. *Cut four.*

Cut four. *Cut four.*

2. **Sew Flying Geese strips.**
   See page 78 for sewing directions.

3. **Cut Flying Geese blocks.**
   Cut four blocks with each background color.
   Sew three flying geese together into rows as shown below.

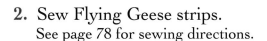

Four blocks. *Four blocks.* *Four blocks.*

4. **Make large triangles.**
   Cut an 8-inch strip from both dark and light fabric.
   Cut each strip into four triangles. See page 11.
   Sew a light and dark triangle together into quilt blocks.

Cut four.

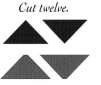

Cut four. *Four blocks.*

5. **Cut center square.**
   Measure the width of the row of three flying geese blocks. Trim the square to this size.

6. **Sew into rows.**
   Choose the design on the right or on the left.
   Sew into three rows, as shown at right.

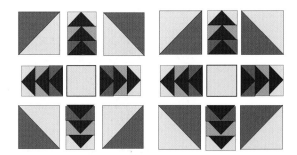

7. **Sew rows together.**

8. **Finish.**
   Layer, quilt, and bind, or make into a pillow.
   Finishing instructions are on page 92.

Chapter *10*
Quilt Strip Blocks

Wildlife, made by Brenda Jonsson. Directions on page 86.

A quilt block can be made from quilt strips.

Shapes, like those shown on page 9, are cut using the 4-angle of the Starmaker 8.

The shapes are then sewn into strips; these are considered quilt blocks.

Strip blocks can be used within the quilt, much like other quilt blocks.

Strip blocks can also be used in sashing and border strips.

Kaye Wood's Strip-Cut Quilts

Quilt Block 22

Triangles are cut using the 4-angle of the Starmaker. The triangles are then sewn into strips, which are considered quilt blocks.

Strip Blocks
Try them as sashing strips in your next quilt.

1. **Cut strips.**
   Cut a strip for each different fabric.
   All strips are the same width.

2. **Cut triangles.**
   Cut the strip by placing the point of the 4-angle of the Starmaker 8 at the top of the strip and cutting. Cut the second triangle by turning the Starmaker 8 upside-down with the point of the 4-angle at the bottom of the strip.

3. **Sew triangles into strips.**
   Sew triangles, right sides together, lining up the edges where they overlap. See the arrows on the diagram.

   Chain-sew into sets of two triangles; chain-sew these into sets of four triangles, etc. Press seam allowances all in the same direction.

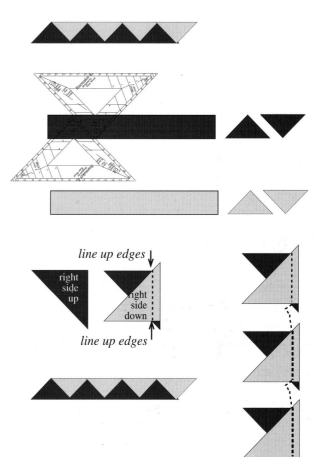

line up edges

right side up

right side down

line up edges

Number of Triangles from Each Strip

Strip width	Triangles
2 inches	19
3 inches	12
4 inches	9
5 inches	7
6 inches	6
7 inches	5
8 inches	4

Flying Ganders

Finished size: 47-by-25 inches

Fabric Requirements

Triangles:

Brown	2/3 yard	Cut seven 3-by-44-inch strips.
Light teal	4 1/4 yard	Cut two 3-by-44-inch strips.
Med. light teal	4 1/4 yard	Cut two 3-by-44-inch strips.
Medium teal	4 1/4 yard	Cut two 3-by-44-inch strips.
Dark teal	4 1/4 yard	Cut two 3-by-44-inch strips.
Border	1/3 yard	Cut five 2-by-44-inch strips.
Backing	48-by-30 inches	
Batting	48-by-30 inches	
Binding	1/4 yard	Cut five 1 3/4-by-44-inch strips.

Make-Believe Flying Geese

Strips of triangles give an interesting variation to the traditional Flying Geese. Try these strips in your quilted clothing or as borders for your next quilt.

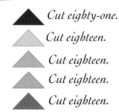

Cut eighty-one.
Cut eighteen.
Cut eighteen.
Cut eighteen.
Cut eighteen.

1. ## Cut triangles.
   Cut eighty-one brown triangles. Cut eighteen triangles from each of the other four fabrics. Follow directions on page 83.

2. ## Sew triangle strips.
   Sew the triangles together into nine identical strips, following the diagram at left. Sewing instructions are on page 83.

3. ## Sew strips together.
   The points of the triangles at the bottom of the row line up with the center of the triangle in the next row.

4. ## Square up the edges.
   Using a ruler, trim both sides to cut off the points.

5. ## Finish.
   Add square or mitered borders, see pages 90 and 91.
   Cut border strips 2 inches wide. Pin-mark at the center and both ends of the border strips. See page 89. Press seam allowances toward the border strip.
   Layer and quilt. See page 92.

Sew nine strips.

Square up both sides.

Quilt Block 23

These pieces are even more topless than the top-less triangles, (page 28), so we'll just call them "shapes."

1. **Cut strips.**
   Using two fabrics, cut three strips all the same width from each fabric.
   The wider the strips, the bigger the trees.

2. **Cut shapes.**
   "A"—Cut "A" shapes with the first line down from the 4-angle on the Starmaker 8 at the top of the strip. Cut the next shape by turning the Starmaker 8 upside-down with the first line down from the 4-angle at the bottom of the strip.

   "B"—Cut "B" shapes by placing the #1 line of the 4-angle of the Starmaker 8 at the top of the strip. Cut the next shape by turning the Starmaker 8 upside-down with the #1 line at the bottom of the strip.

   "C"—Cut "C" shapes by placing the #2 line of the 4-angle of the Starmaker 8 at the top of the strip. Cut the next shape by turning the Starmaker 8 upside-down with the #2 line at the bottom of the strip.

3. **Sew into strips.**
   Sew the shapes, right sides together, with a 3/8-inch seam allowance, lining up the edges as shown on the diagram at right.
   Chain-sew into sets of two shapes; chain-sew these into sets of four shapes, etc. Press seam allowances of the top and bottom strips away from the smallest shape.

4. **Sew strips together.**
   Sew strips, right sides together, using 1/4-inch seam allowances, matching the centers of each shape.

Trees are great for borders!
The secret is sewing the pieces into strips using 3/8-inch seam allowances.

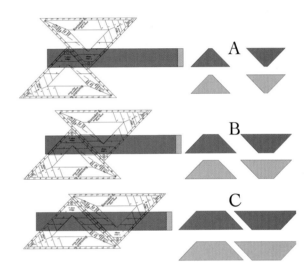

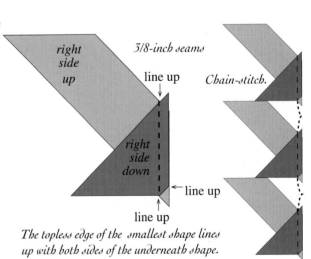

The topless edge of the smallest shape lines up with both sides of the underneath shape.

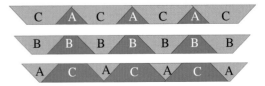

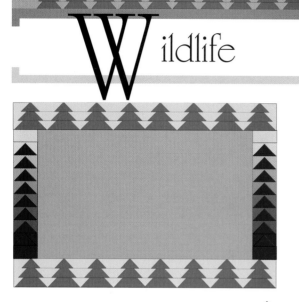

Wildlife

Finished size: 52 1/2-by-34 inches
A photo of this quilt, made by
Brenda Jonsson, is on page 82.

Fabric Requirements

Large print	Approximately 25-by-42 inches.	
Flying Geese		
Brown	1/4 yard	Cut two 3-by-44-inch strips.
Background	Eight gradated shades of teal.	
	From each, cut one 3-by-12 inches.	
Tree strip block		
Green	1/2 yard	Cut eight 2-by-44-inch strips.
Background	1/2 yard	Cut eight 2-by-44-inch strips.
Backing	55-by-38 inches	
Batting	55-by-38 inches	
Binding	1/3 yard	Cut five 1 3/4-inch strips.

1. **Make Flying Geese border.**
   Directions are on page 78. Cut sixteen triangles from the brown (geese) fabric strips. Cut two background triangles from each of the eight shades of teal strips.

   Sew Flying Geese strips. Directions are on page 78.
   Sew a strip of two geese and two topless triangles of the same color together.
   Cut Flying Geese blocks; two with each background color.
   Sew two geese vertical rows, each with eight geese, shaded from light to dark.
   Measure the side of the large print. More geese can be added to make a longer border, or add an equal amount of fabric to the top and bottom of the row of geese to make the border fit the print, as shown.
   Sew geese rows to each side of the large print.

Cut sixteen.
Cut two.
Cut two.
Cut two.
Cut two.
Cut two.
Cut two.
Cut two.
Cut two.

2. **Put together tree border.**
   Directions are on page 86. Cut eighteen "A," eighteen "B," and eighteen "C" shapes from green.
   Cut sixteen "A," sixteen "B," and sixteen "C" shapes from the background.

   Sew into six rows, each with nine green shapes and eight blue shapes:
   • two rows with "A" and "C" shapes
   • two rows with "B" and "B" shapes
   • two rows with "C" and "A" shapes
   Add more shapes for a longer border.
   Sew rows together, matching center of shapes.
   Sew a tree border to the top and bottom of the large print.
   Trim the ends even with the rows of geese.

Cut eighteen each. 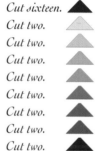 A B C *Cut sixteen each.*

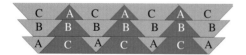

3. **Layer, quilt, and bind. See page 92.**

Chapter 11

Finishing Techniques

Scrap Happy Pillow, made by Kaye Wood. Directions on page 40.

Yardages for Quilt Blocks

All yardages given with projects are for strips cut 42 or 44 inches (across the width of the fabric).

To make any of these quilts larger or smaller, or to plan your very own quilt, use these charts.

To figure the amount of fabric needed for your special quilt, count the number of triangles in your design. The charts below tell you how many triangles you can cut from one 42/44-inch strip of fabric.

Square Up the Quilt Blocks

Each square in your project needs to be the same size. You can measure each quilt block by stacking a few at a time. They will probably be all the same. If they are the same, congratulations!

If they are not the same size, don't worry; just square up the blocks. To square up the blocks, use a square ruler that is larger than your block and has a diagonal line from corner to corner.

Place the square ruler on the block with the diagonal line of the ruler on the seamline between the two triangles.

If your block should be 8 inches, line up the 8-inch square lines on the ruler with two sides of the block.

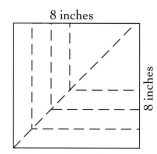
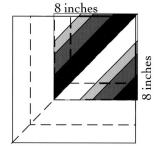

If the block measures less than the 8 inches, move the ruler so the 7 3/4-inch lines line up with two edges of the block. If this size will work, trim all your blocks to this size. If it is necessary to trim some or all of the blocks, it is best to trim a little equally on all four sides.

Yardages and Sizes for Quilt Blocks 1, 2, 3, 4, 6, 7, 9, 10 and 11

combination strip width	triangles per 44-inch strip	block size	finished size
3 inches	13*	4 1/4 inches	3 3/4 inches
4 inches	10	5 5/8 inches	5 1/8 inches
5 inches	7*	7 3/4 inches	7 1/4 inches
6 inches	6	8 inches	7 1/2 inches
7 inches	5*	9 1/2 inches	9 inches
8 inches	4	10 1/2 inches	10 inches
8 1/2 inches	4	11 1/2 inches	11 inches

Yardages and Sizes for Spool Quilt Blocks 5 and 8

combination strip width	triangles per 44-inch strip	block size	finished size
3 inches	13*	5 1/4 inches	4 3/4 inches
4 inches	10	7 1/4 inches	6 3/4 inches
5 inches	7*	9 1/4 inches	8 3/4 inches
6 inches	6	11 inches	10 1/2 inches
7 inches	5*	13 inches	12 1/2 inches
8 inches	4	15 1/2 inches	15 inches
8 1/2 inches	4	16-1/2 inches	16 inches

*When cutting an uneven number of triangles, cut the second strip beginning with the triangle you have the least of.

Sashing Strips

Pin-marking

Most of the these quilt blocks will have bias outside edges. Pin-marking is used to control the bias when adding sashing strips, or when we add the first border.

Short Sashing Strips *(between quilt blocks)*

1. Measure the quilt blocks. Square up the blocks, if necessary; see page 88.

2. Cut sashing strips the exact length (size of the block). Sizes are given with each project, but measure your block because your sashing strip has to match your block.

3. Sew the sashing strips. Line up the top of the sashing strip and the top of the block. Start sewing with the sashing strip on top to control the stretch. After about an inch of sewing, stop and match up the bottom of the sashing strip with the bottom of the block.

Continue sewing.

Chain-stitch from one block to the next.

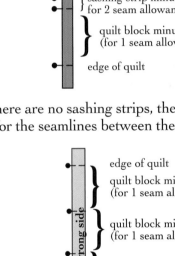

Chain-stitch: Sew from one block to the next without cutting threads.

Press the seam allowances toward the sashing strip.

Long Sashing Strips and Borders *(between rows or for the first border)*

1. Cut horizontal sashing and border strips across the width (40 or 44 inches wide). If necessary, sew sashing strips together to make a longer strip.

On small quilts, vertical sashing and border strips can be cut across the width of the fabric.

Vertical sashing strips and borders on large quilts should be cut lengthwise on the fabric. Cut the length of the sashing strip at least 4 inches longer than needed. For mitered corners, allow more.

2. Pin-Mark sashing/border strips to quilt blocks with bias edges. Pin-Marking the sashing and border strips will control the stretch in the bias edges. The pins will match up with the seamlines in the row of quilt blocks.

Place a pin in the center of the long sashing strip. If the sashing strip has been pieced together, the center pin should be on the seamline.

From the center pin, measure and pin-mark along the left-hand side of the strip by placing pins that will line up with seamlines and both ends, as shown at below. The center pin should line up with a seamline.

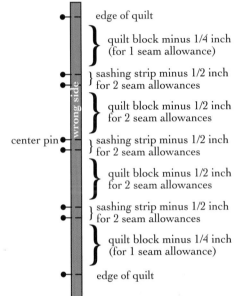

edge of quilt

quilt block minus 1/4 inch (for 1 seam allowance)

sashing strip minus 1/2 inch for 2 seam allowances

quilt block minus 1/2 inch for 2 seam allowances

center pin — sashing strip minus 1/2 inch for 2 seam allowances

quilt block minus 1/2 inch for 2 seam allowances

sashing strip minus 1/2 inch for 2 seam allowances

quilt block minus 1/4 inch (for 1 seam allowance)

edge of quilt

If there are no sashing strips, the pin-marks will be for the seamlines between the quilt blocks.

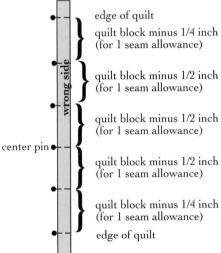

edge of quilt

quilt block minus 1/4 inch (for 1 seam allowance)

quilt block minus 1/2 inch (for 1 seam allowance)

quilt block minus 1/2 inch (for 1 seam allowance)

center pin — quilt block minus 1/2 inch (for 1 seam allowance)

quilt block minus 1/4 inch (for 1 seam allowance)

edge of quilt

For borders and sashing strips on straight of grain edges, like the Spool Blocks or any second border, pins only need to mark the center, the ends, and halfway between the center and the ends of the strip.

3. Sew the right side of the sashing strip to one side of each row. Sew with the sashing strip on top to avoid stretching the bias edges.

Match pins to seamlines, but <u>do not</u> pin the sashing strip to the quilt blocks, and <u>do not</u> remove pins.

Press seam allowances toward the sashing strip.

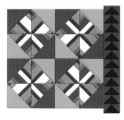

4. Sew rows together by matching the pins on the left side of each sashing strip to the seamlines. Remove the pins as you come to the matching seamline. Trim the ends of the sashing strips even with the blocks.

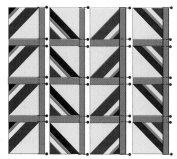

Border strips are pin-marked in the same way.

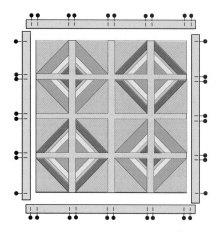

Borders

One or more borders can be added to adjust the finished size of the quilt and to frame the edges. Borders should be in scale with the rest of the quilt and should enhance the design. It is better to use two or more borders, than to make a wide border, unless the wide border is an interesting stripe.

Pieced Borders

Make the quilt fit the border. There are lots of ideas in this book for making pieced borders, but how do you make a pieced border that will fit your quilt? It is easier to enlarge the quilt to fit the border. After the quilt is pieced, make the pieced border strips. If the pieced border is too long, add a border strip to the quilt to make the size right. For example, if the quilt top is 36 inches high and the border strip is 40 inches high, add a top and bottom border to make the quilt fit the border.

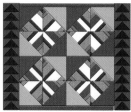

If the top and bottom pieced border strips are too long, add borders to each side to make the quilt fit the border. If the border strips are too short, add solid squares to make them longer.

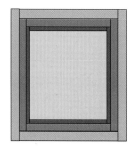

Square Borders

Cut the top and bottom border strips the width of the quilt. Pin-mark both ends and the center and sew to the quilt, with the border strip on top. Press the seam allowances toward the border strips.

Measure, pin-mark, and sew the side border strips. Press the seam allowances toward the borders.

Mitered Borders

Add the top and bottom borders.
Cut the border strips the width of the quilt plus a 1-inch extension on each side, i.e. if the border is 2 inches wide, cut the border strip the width of the quilt plus 6 inches (*2-inch border + 1 inch = 3 inches x two ends = 6 inches*).

If several borders will be mitered, sew the border strips together first; then sew to quilt as if it is just one border.

1. Pin the strip to the quilt at the center and end points, leaving an extension at each end. Sew from edge to edge of the quilt. Press the seam allowances toward the border strip.

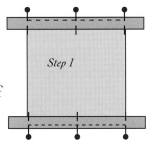

Step 1

Sewing two of the border strips all the way from edge to edge will lock in the corners and make the miters easier.

2. Add the side borders. Cut the side strips the length of the quilt plus an extension (the width of the border plus 1 inch) at both ends. Pin the

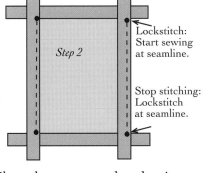

Step 2

Lockstitch: Start sewing at seamline.

Stop stitching: Lockstitch at seamline.

strip to the quilt at the center and end points, leaving an extension at both ends.
Lockstitch (3 or 4 stitches in one place) and start sewing at the seamline of the top border (do not backstitch to lock). Sew to the seamline of the bottom and lockstitch. Press seam allowances toward the border strip.

3. Trim the ends of the border strips even with each other. This will help you to miter the corners.

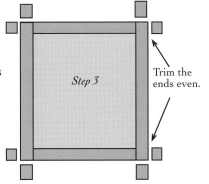

Step 3

Trim the ends even.

4. Fold the quilt diagonally, right sides together. The seam allowances should be toward the quilt and away from the border strips.
Pin both border strips together carefully along the seamlines on both sides of the diagonal stitching line. Lockstitch and start sewing at the seamline, and sew to the outside corner. Press the miter. Trim off the extra fabric in the seam allowance.

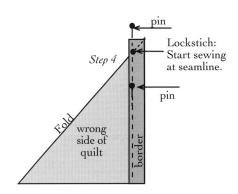

pin

Lockstich: Start sewing at seamline.

Step 4

pin

Fold

wrong side of quilt

border

Eyelet Edging

Eyelet is sewn, right sides together, to the quilt top. The band, or gathered part of the eyelet, should be even with the outside of the quilt. If your eyelet has a fabric band, you can get a nice full corner by removing about 9 inches of the eyelet band at the corner. Run a basting stitch by hand or machine where the band was removed. Gather the eyelet; then sew around the corner.

Envelopes or Pillowcase Finish

Cut a backing piece and batting the same size as the pieced top. Pin the top and backing, right sides together, with the batting underneath. Sew around the quilt, leaving an opening along one edge to turn the quilt right sides out. Turn right side out. Close the opening with hand stitches.

Get Ready to Quilt

There are several ways to finish your quilt: quilting by hand, quilting by home sewing machine, quilting on a professional quilting machine, hand tying or machine tying.

Professional quilting machine—Before sending your quilt top out to be quilted, take a look at a sample of the quilters work. Ask questions, such as can they do free motion quilting, pattern quilting, and straight or diagonal stitching? Who will furnish the batting and backing? Who will plan the quilting design? I send all of my quilts out to be machine-quilted on the American Professional Quilting System machine.

Batting

Batting comes in several different thicknesses—very thin to comforter thickness. Be sure to get the weight of batting that will give you the finish you want for your quilt. If you're not sure, go with the thinnest available. Remove the batting from the package the day before you use it, or put the batting in the dryer (no heat) for several minutes to allow it to breathe.

Backing Fabric

Backing fabric can be a plain muslin or a printed fabric. Quilt blocks can even be sewn together for a backing. If you are hand quilting, choose an all-cotton fabric for the backing; it will be easier to quilt. Backing fabrics can be pieced from one or more fabrics.

Layer the Quilt

To layer a quilt means to stack three layers (top, batting, backing) together. Cut the backing and batting approximately 4 inches larger than the finished top. The backing of the quilt should be held taut by using a quilt frame or by taping the fabric, right side down, to a flat surface, such as the floor or a pingpong table. The batting is laid on top of the backing; smooth the batting out but don't stretch it. The quilt top is placed right side up over the batting.

Hold the layers together

There are several ways to keep the layers (top, batting, backing) together: hand baste, safety pin baste or use a spray adhesive to hold the layers together.

A. Safety pin baste

Use small rust-proof safety pins. While the backing is still taped to a flat surface, insert but do not close the safety pins. After all the pins are in place, remove the tape from the backing and close the safety pins.

B. Spray adhesive

Spray adhesive eliminates the need for hand basting or safety pin basting. After the quilt back is held securely in place, spray the wrong side with a spray adhesive. Place the batting, and pat it in place. Spray the top side of the batting and place the quilt top, wrong side down, on top of the batting. Machine or hand quilt.

Machine Tie

To machine tie a quilt, drop or cover the feed dogs and set the machine for a zigzag stitch. Choose a washable yarn or use pearl cotton. Lay the yarn on top of the quilt. Take several zigzag stitches over the yarn. Tie in a knot or bow. If you want bows, tie the yarn into a bow before zigzagging over it.

Machine Quilting

To machine quilt, use an even-feed foot, lock your stitches, and use matching thread, decorative thread or invisible thread in the needle. Bring the bobbin thread through to the top of the quilt. Hold both bobbin and top thread. The bobbin thread should match the quilt back or the needle thread. Try a sample first; the stitch length is determined by the loft of the batting—lengthen if necessary.

Hanging Sleeve

Cut fabric 8 inches wide and 2 inches shorter than the width of the quilt. Turn the short ends under a 1/2 inch and topstitch. Press the strip in half (4 inches wide). Sew the raw edges of the sleeve to the top edge of the quilt. Hand stitch the folded edge 4 inches down from the top of the quilt.

For hanging tabs, cut 4-by-8-inch pieces, and attach several to the top of the quilt.

Binding

A binding finishes off the edges and frames the quilt. Binding strips can be cut on the straight of grain or on the bias. I prefer a straight-of-grain double binding. The finished binding (the width showing on the quilt top) can be very narrow to extra wide. However, the seam allowance must be the same width as the finished binding. If the finished binding is a 1/2 inch, then the seam allowance must be a 1/2 inch because the binding must be padded with the edge of the quilt. If you use a finished binding wider than 1/4 inch, the width of your last border may need to be adjusted; if your finished binding is 1 1/2 inches, the seam allowance will be 1 1/2 inches, and the last border will be 1 1/2 inches narrower than it is cut.

To use a double binding, cut the binding strips six times the finished width of the binding, i.e. if the finished width is 1/2 inch, the strip would be cut 3 inches wide, except when the finished binding is 1/4 inch, the strip needs to be cut 1 3/4 inches, as shown.

Double Binding	
Finished binding	Cut Strip
1/4 inch	1-3/4 inch
1/2 inch	3 inch
3/4 inch	4-1/2 inch
1 inch	6 inch
1-1/2 inch	9 inch

Cut enough binding strips to go around the quilt plus 12 inches. Sew two or more binding strips together on the diagonal (bias).

At the beginning of the strip, fold the end diagonally, and press a crease.

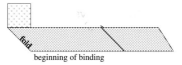
beginning of binding

Fold the binding strip in half, wrong sides together, and press.

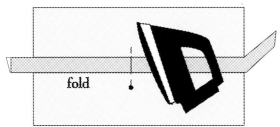

fold

To quickly get a folded strip:
Fold one end of the strip.
Put a pin in the ironing pad and up over the strip and into the pad.
Pull the folded strip under the pin and under an iron.

Sew the raw edges of the binding strip even with the edge of the quilt top. Leave a 6-inch tail at the beginning of the binding and start sewing on one side of the quilt—never at the corner. Sew with both raw edges of the binding even with the edge of the quilt.

Mitered Corners

To "perfect miter" the corners:

Step 1: Sew to a seam allowance width from the next side of the quilt. With the needle in the quilt, pivot and sew diagonally to the corner of the quilt. This forms a sewn-in miter.

Step 2: Fold the binding strip up so it lines up with the next side of the quilt.

Mitered Corners

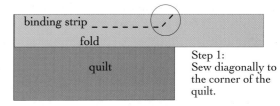
binding strip
fold
quilt

Step 1:
Sew diagonally to the corner of the quilt.

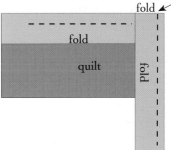
fold
quilt
fold

Step 2:
Fold the binding strip up at right angles along the diagonally sewn line, so it will line up with the next side of the quilt.

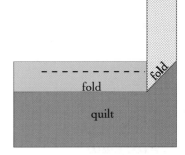
fold
quilt
fold
fold

Step 3:
Fold the binding strip down and start sewing at the folded edge, a seam allowance in from the side.

Step 3: Bring the binding strip down even with the next side. Start stitching from the edge of the quilt. Sew to the next corner. After mitering the last corner, lay the beginning and ending of the strip together. Fold a crease in the ending. Bring the folded crease lines right sides together, pin, and sew.

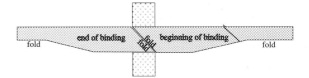
fold   end of binding   beginning of binding   fold

Strip Like A Pro
Strip-Quilting Books, Videos and Master Templates by Kaye Wood

Books

Quilt Like A Pro • *Turn Me Over—I'm Reversible* • *Serger Patchwork Projects*
Starmakers Ablaze 1—Log Cabin Triangles • *Starmakers Ablaze 2—Log Cabin Diamonds*
Savage Star • *6 Hour Quilt* book and video • *TwinStar Jacket* • *Stardust Quilt*
Strip Quilting Projects • *Strip Quilting Projects 2* • *Strip Quilting Projects 3* • *Strip Quilting Projects 4*
Strip Quilting Projects 5 • *Strip Quilting Projects 6* • *Strip Quilting Projects 7*
Strip Quilting Projects 8 • *Strip Quilting Projects 9* • *Strip Quilting Projects 10*
Easy Hexagon Designs book and video • *Fantastic Fans and Wedge Designs* book and video

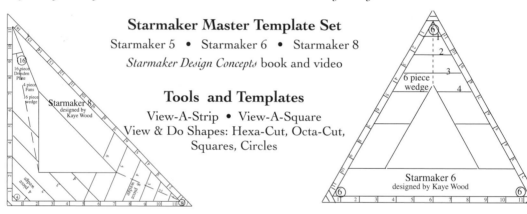

Starmaker Master Template Set
Starmaker 5 • Starmaker 6 • Starmaker 8
Starmaker Design Concepts book and video

Tools and Templates
View-A-Strip • View-A-Square
View & Do Shapes: Hexa-Cut, Octa-Cut,
Squares, Circles

Other products that Kaye uses in her strip-quilting:

Rulers

Static Stickers

Spray Adhesive

Rotary cutter/mat

Frames for mounting quilt blocks

1/4-inch foot for the sewing machine

The quilts in this book were machine-quilted by:

Marilyn Badger
Carol Moss
Oregon Coast Quilting
(541) 412-1002

Nancy Webster
Northwoods Quilting
Waters, Michigan
(517) 731-5166

Jane Ehinger
West Branch, Michigan

The Cotton Patch
Tawas, Michigan
(517) 362-6779

Glossary

4-angle: One of the three angles of the Starmaker 8 Master Template.

Backing: Back of the quilt.

Batting: Filler that goes in between the quilt top and backing.

Bias edges: 45 degree angle from the straight of grain.

Binding: A narrow strip that goes around the outside edge of a quilt.

Border strips: One or more strips added to the outside edge of a quilt.

Chain-sew: Sew from one piece of fabric to the next without cutting threads.

Combination strip: Two or more strips sewn together to be cut into shapes.

Crosscut: Cut across the combination strip.

Envelope finish: Right sides of the quilt and backing are sewn together, and then turned right side out.

Fat quarters: A yard of fabric that is cut in half horizontally and vertically, approximately 18-by-22 inches.

Flying Geese: A quilt block made from triangles and background fabrics.

Fussy-cuts: A fabric design centered inside a shape.

Horizontal: Sideways; even with the horizon.

Layer: To put the quilt top, batting and backing together.

Lockstitch: Stitch in one place to lock stitches.

Machine tie: Tie the quilt with yarn or cord, instead of quilting.

Mitered bindings: Folding the binding at the corners so the seam is diagonal.

Mitered borders: Sewing the borders so the corner seam is diagonal.

Motifs: A fabric design.

On point: Quilt turned so the blocks are turned at a 45-degree angle.

Pillowcase finish: Same as envelope finish.

Pin-mark: Pinning sashing strips and borders to match seamlines.

Pointless designs: Designs that don't have points to match; perfect for beginners.

Quilt: Any project that is made from fabric and layered.

Quilt strip blocks: Strips of fabric that are quilt blocks.

Rotary cutting: Using a rotary cutting wheel, mat and ruler to cut strips.

Sashing strips: Strips of fabric that separate quilt blocks and rows of quilt blocks.

Scant 1/4-inch seam allowance: Slightly less than 1/4 inch; with the turn of the cloth, exactly 1/2 inch (1/4 inch x two fabrics) is taken off for each seam.

Selvedge: The woven edges of the fabric.

Serge: Use a serger machine to seam and finish edges.

Sleeve: A strip of fabric attached to the back of the quilt to allow a pole to be inserted to hang the quilt.

Spool blocks: Blocks made from 4 triangles; the design resembles a spool of thread.

Starmaker 8 Master Template: One of three master templates that simplify cutting.

Static Sticker: Transparent plastic that sticks to rulers to use as a guide.

Straight of grain: The lengthwise or crosswise threads of the fabric.

Tube-sewing: Sewing two strips of fabric, right sides together, along both long edges.

Vertical: Up and down.

Zigzag: A sewing machine stitch that moves back and forth as it forms the stitch.

Index